Classroom Computer Center

Grades 5–6

By Concetta Doti Ryan, M.A.

Illustrated by Dave McPeek

HyperStudio® is a registered trademark of Roger Wagner Publishing, Inc.

Screen Shots from System 8.1© 1983-1997 Apple Computer, Inc. Used with permission.
ClarisWorks software Copyright 1991–1997 Apple Computer, Inc.
Apple® and the Apple logo, and *ClarisWorks* are trademarks of Apple Computer, Inc.,
registered in the U.S. and other countries. All Rights Reserved.

At the time of printing *ClarisWorks software* is named *AppleWorks software.*

Project Manager: Barbara G. Hoffman
Editor: Vicky Shiotsu
Book Design: Anthony D. Paular
Cover Design: Anthony D. Paular
Pre-Press Production: Daniel Willits

FS123297 Classroom Computer Center Grades 5–6
All rights reserved—Printed in the U.S.A.
Cat. No. FS123297
ISBN 0-7862-0206-X
23740 Hawthorne Blvd.
Torrance, CA 90505

Table of Contents

Learning centers have been used by teachers in primary classrooms for years. Some activities students complete at learning centers are designed to practice and reinforce skills. Because students are already familiar with the skills, they can complete the practice activities at the centers on their own without teacher intervention.

Traditional classroom learning centers include a reading center, a writing center, a math center, a science center, a listening center, and an art center. Now that you have a computer in the classroom, students have the opportunity to enjoy a whole new center! A computer learning center encourages students to familiarize themselves with the computer and practice a variety of skills on their own.

Computer Learning Activities

The activities in this book are based on the *ClarisWorks* and *HyperStudio* programs. *ClarisWorks* includes the following features: word processing, drawing and painting, and spreadsheets. *HyperStudio* is a multimedia tool that allows users to present a variety of presentations that employ graphics, sounds, and special effects. The only equipment needed is a computer and printer. A color printer works best.

The activities are designed to be completed during a single 25-minute sitting. Each activity includes a lesson plan for the teacher and an activity page for students. The activity pages should be reproduced and glued onto heavy paper to make activity cards; the cards could be laminated to make them more durable. The activity cards are designed to be placed at the computer learning center to help guide students through each activity. In many cases, illustrations on each activity card help students see what the end results might look like.

Student Rotation

Students move to the computer learning center just as they do to the other centers in your classroom. If the computer is the only center you will be using, then schedule the students in 25-minute blocks throughout the week. If you find that you do not have enough time to give each students a 25-minute block, try using 20-minute blocks, or have the students work in pairs. If parent volunteers or older students are available, ask them to be "computer buddies" at your center. These "buddies" can help familiarize your class with the computer and the particular software, and they can also help move students to the center.

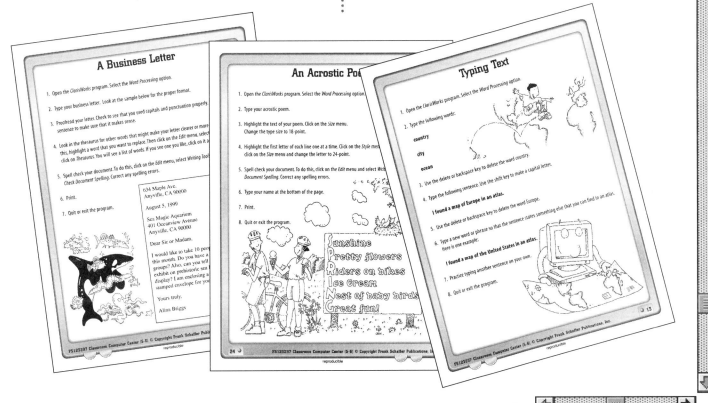

Center Management

The lessons in this book incorporate special features to help your center run smoothly and efficiently.

1. At the end of each activity card, students are asked to exit or quit the program so that the computer is always left ready for the next student.

2. For activities to be printed, students are prompted to type their names on their work to make assessing and distributing the papers easy.

3. Assessment criteria are included with every lesson should you decide to give a grade or a score.

4. In some lessons, students are asked to save their work. Always give students a name for the file and have them add their initials. For example, you may ask students to save the file as *story.their initials*.

6. The technology prerequisites for each lesson are listed. A basic introduction to *ClarisWorks* or *HyperStudio* prior to engaging in any of the lessons in this book will provide students with the basic skills necessary to complete the activities.

Introducing Software

The best way to introduce a piece of software to students is to demonstrate it. If you have access to a large screen projection device, you can project what you are doing on your computer onto a movie screen. Or, you may have access to a device which allows you to project what you are doing on your computer onto a television. If you do not have a projection device, you can rotate students in small groups and show them how to use the software as they join you at the computer.

Once students have been introduced to the software, allow them some time at the computer center to play and become familiar with the tools. If you do not allow exploration time, students will have a difficult time focusing on the activities they are to complete because they will spend time experimenting with the tools. After students have had at least one or two center sessions where they are allowed to explore the software, they will be ready to complete the activities included in this book.

The activities in this book will help you meet the challenge of preparing your students for a world that is increasingly dependent on computer technology. As you implement the ideas in this book, you will find your students gaining important computer skills and enjoying computers as a fun, rewarding, and meaningful part of their lives.

In order to do the activities in this book, students need to know some basic computer operations. Briefly introduce each item on the list below to your students so that they can work independently.

HARDWARE

The Screen

The screen is the face of the monitor. When the computer is turned on, it will give you a list of programs called a menu. Often the screen will have small pictures that accompany a program name. These pictures are called icons.

The Mouse

The mouse is the small device attached to the computer that creates an arrow or similar symbol on the screen. This arrow is called a cursor. Moving the mouse to the left moves the cursor on the computer screen to the left; moving the mouse to the right moves the cursor to the right.

To select programs and tools within programs, move the cursor directly onto the icon or word, and click once.

Double-clicking the mouse means clicking twice in rapid succession on the mouse button. *ClarisWorks* and *HyperStudio* are opened by double-clicking the mouse on the appropriate icon.

The Keyboard

Important keys to know on the keyboard include the return or enter key, the space bar, the shift key, and the delete or backspace key.

- **Return or Enter key**: moves the cursor to the next line (like the carriage return on a typewriter)

- **Space Bar**: makes a space (like the space bar on a typewriter)

- **Shift Key**: selects a second function for the key (such as capital letters or a symbol)

- **Delete or Backspace Key**: is used for backspacing and/or correcting errors

SOFTWARE

ClarisWorks

Open the program and click on the *Word Processing*, *Painting*, or *Spreadsheet* options as directed in the activity. To quit or exit, click on the *File* menu and select *Quit* or *Exit*.

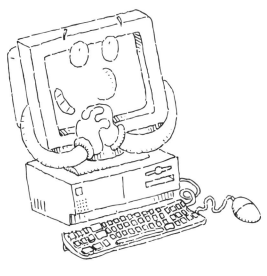

HyperStudio

Open the program and click on the *New Stack* option to begin creating a new card. To quit or exit, click on the *File* menu and select *Quit* or *Exit*.

PRINTING

In both programs, click on the *File* menu and then click on *Print*.

When you open the *ClarisWorks* program, you are prompted to select among six options. For the activities in this book, students will select *Painting*, *Word Processing*, or *Spreadsheet*.

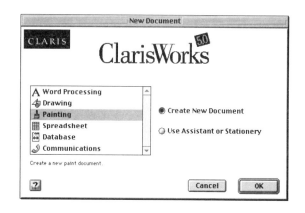

Painting

A tool palette appears when the *Painting* option is selected. Below is a description of the tools they will use with the activities in this book. The lessons on pages 13–15 give guided practice with the specific tools.

The text tool looks like a capital *A*. This tool is selected for typing text.

The line tool looks like diagonal line. It is used for making lines.

The shape tools are used for making various shapes. These tools include the rectangle, rounded rectangle, oval, arc, and polygon.

The brush tool is located near the bottom of the tool panel. It is used to paint strokes of various thicknesses.

The pencil tool is used for drawing free-form lines.

The paint can is used for filling an enclosed are with colors and patterns. It is important to remind students that when filling in an area with color, they must position the tip of the can so that it touches the enclosed area.

The spray can "sprays" color onto the screen.

The eraser tool is used to remove part of a picture.

The large rectangular shape beside the paint can near the bottom of the tool panel indicates what color or pattern has been selected for painting. For example, if the rectangle is blue, the brush tool will automatically produce blue strokes.

The rectangular shape beside the pen at the very bottom of the tool panel indicates what color or pattern has been selected for lines and borders of objects. For example, if the rectangle shows red lines, a shape tool will produce shapes with red borders.

FS123297 Classroom Computer Center (5-6) © Copyright Frank Schaffer Publications, Inc.

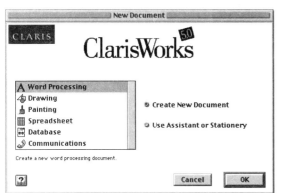

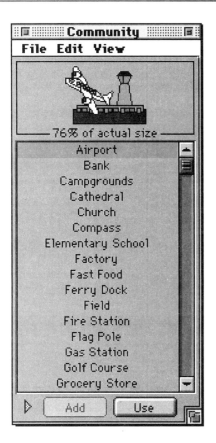

Word Processing

When the *Word Processing* option is selected, the cursor automatically appears at the top of the left-hand portion of the screen. The menus at the top of the screen allow you to change the font, size, and style of text used.

To change a font, click on the *Font* menu and then select from any of the fonts listed. To change the size of the font, click on the *Size* menu and then choose the sizes available. To make text bold, italic, or underlined, click on the *Style* menu and choose the appropriate description.

Library

For several of the lessons in this book, students are directed to use the *Library* and add graphics to their work. To do this, click on the *File* menu and select *Library*. A list of topics will appear. Choose a topic, such as *Community*. Once a topic is selected, a list of graphics will appear. Select a graphic and click *Use*. The graphic will appear on the screen. If you are working in the *Painting* option, move the graphic into the desired position by clicking on it while holding down the mouse button and moving it. If you are working in the *Word Processing* option, the graphic acts like a piece of text. To move it, place the cursor before the graphic and press the space bar or return key to position the picture in place. To make the graphic smaller or larger, click on the small box in the right-hand bottom corner and drag inward or outward.

How to Use *ClarisWorks*

Spreadsheet

For some of the activities in this book, students will be using the *Spreadsheet* option in *ClarisWorks*. A spreadsheet is a tool that can make a variety of calculations. It is often used to chart, organize, and analyze information. A spreadsheet is made up of rows and columns. Rows are horizontal and numbered along the left side. Columns are vertical and labeled across the top with letters. Each rectangle within the spreadsheet is called a cell. Each cell contains words, numbers, or formulas. When working with formulas, as you make changes in the cell data, you automatically see how the changes affect the end results.

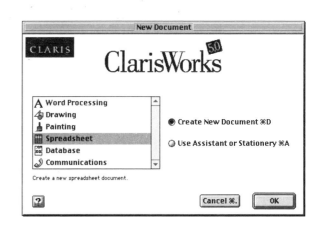

Spreadsheets can also have headers (titles). To create a header, click on the *Format* menu and select *Insert Header*. Then type the header for the spreadsheet.

The letters across the top of the spreadsheet indicate the columns. In this book, students will be working with columns A–D. The rows of the spreadsheet are numbered. Students will be working with rows 1–10. To enter data or a formula, you need to click inside the appropriate cell and start typing. What is typed appears in the entry bar. When the ✔ is clicked, the entry appears in the cell. Clicking the *x* cancels the entry.

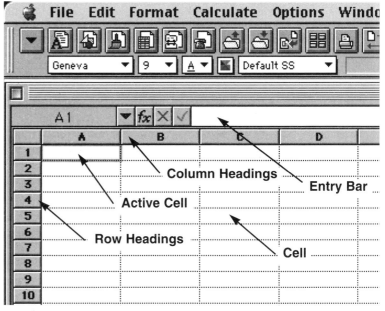

Spreadsheets and formulas help you make calculations easily and quickly. Formulas are entered in a specific manner. They always begin with the equal sign (=), followed by the computation to be performed. The following symbols are used: + (addition), – (subtraction), * (multiplication), / (division).

Examples: =4+2   means 4 + 2

=4–2   means 4 – 2

=4*2   means 4 x 2

=4/2   means 4 ÷ 2

The lessons in this book will familiarize students with spreadsheets and give them opportunities to experiment with formulas and other kinds of cell data.

ClarisWorks offers many features that allow students to explore, create, and experiment. As students work through the lessons in this book, they will become confident computer users and will be eager to create documents on their own.

HyperStudio is a tool for creating multimedia presentations. Many of its features work similarly to a painting program, such as the one offered in *ClarisWorks*.

Cards and Stacks

A *HyperStudio* multimedia presentation is made up of individual cards. Each screen is essentially a card. When the student creates two or more cards, it is referred to as a *stack*. In some of the lessons in this book, students create only one card. Other lessons require students to create a stack.

When you first open *HyperStudio*, click on *New Stack* in order to create a new file. To view a stack you have made and saved previously, click on *Open Stack*.

Tools

The tool palette in *HyperStudio* does not automatically appear on the screen. It is retrieved by clicking on the *Tools* menu and dragging it to the side of the page. The tools are similar to those used in other painting programs—the paintbrush, spray can, paint can, eraser, line tool, pencil, shape tools, and text tool (*T*). The colors of the tools are changed by clicking on the *Colors* menu.

The tools at the top of the tool palette are for editing. The *B* edit tool edits any buttons that have been created on a card. (Buttons are used for adding sounds, graphics, and special effects.) The *G* edit tool edits graphics. The megaphone edits sound. The *T* edit tool edits text. The arrow selects objects that you want to move or change. The hand tool is used for clicking on buttons so that you can move around within a stack.

Adding Text

You can add text directly onto the card using the text tool. If the text tool is used to type in text, the text is essentially "painted" onto the card and cannot be changed unless the eraser tool is used to erase the entire text. You can also add text using a *text object*. A text object is a box, or frame, that holds text in place. The text inside this box can be edited with the *T* edit tool.

To add a text object (box or frame), click on the *Objects* menu and select *Add a Text Object*. A box appears on the card. This "text box" will hold the text you want to place on the card. To resize the box, move the cursor onto the frame until an arrow appears; move the arrow to change the box to the desired size. To move the box, click on it and drag it into position.

How to Use *HyperStudio*

To format the text appearance, click anywhere on the screen. A dialog box appears and you will see a highlighted box. This box lets you type in a name for the text box that you will create. To pick a color for the text and one for the background, click on the colors in the designated boxes at the left of the screen.

To format the text, click on *Style*. Another dialog box appears, allowing you to choose a font, style, size, and alignment for the text. Once you make your selections, click *OK* on all the dialog boxes. You can then start typing the text.

Text Appearance

Text

Background

HyperStudio Sample Text

Get File...

Actions...

Cancel

Name: Untitled

☑ Draw scroll bar   ☐ Read only
☑ Scrollable   ☑ Draw frame

Style...

OK

Working With Buttons

To link individual cards to create a multimedia presentation, you need to add buttons. Buttons are designated by words and/or graphics.

Adding Buttons

To add a button, click on the *Objects* menu and select *Add a Button*. A dialog box appears. First choose a shape for the button. Then in the *Name* box, type the text that you want to see on your button.

Objects
Add a Button...	⌘B
Add a Graphic Object...	⌘G
Add a Text Object...	⌘T
Hypertext Links...	⌘L
Bring Closer	⌘+
Send Farther	⌘-
About this Card...	
About this Stack...	

Adding Graphics to Buttons

Add a graphic to a button by clicking on *Icons* or *Show Icon*. A screen appears with icons on it. Click on the icon you want and then click *OK*.

Adding Color

Next, use the color palette at the side of the screen to select the color you want for the words on the button. Select a different color for the background. Click *OK*, and the button appears on the card. To move the button into place, click on it and drag it.

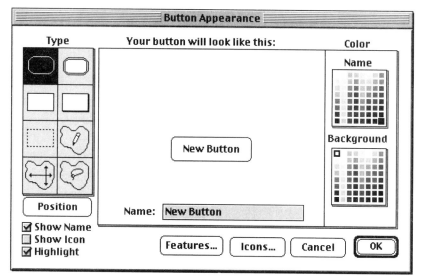

Button Appearance

Type   Your button will look like this: Color

Name

New Button

Background

Position

☑ Show Name
☐ Show Icon
☑ Highlight

Name: New Button

Features...   Icons...   Cancel   OK

FS123297 Classroom Computer Center (5-6) © Copyright Frank Schaffer Publications, Inc.

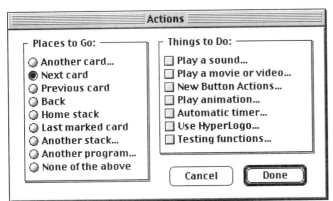

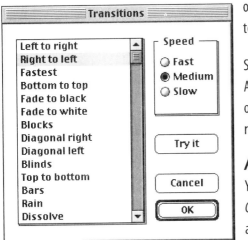

Adding Actions

Next, click anywhere on the screen to add the button "actions." A dialog box appears labeled *Actions*. Actions are sounds and/or special effects that occur when the button is pressed.

First look at the *Places to Go* box and select *Next card.* This indicates that you are setting up the button on your card so that once you press it, the next card in your stack will appear. When you select *Next card,* a box labeled *Transitions* appears. A transition is a special effect that takes place when you press the button and move from one card to the next. You will see a list of transitions. Choose one and then click *OK* to return to the dialog box labeled *Actions.*

Sounds are added to your button by clicking on *Play a Sound* in the *Things to Do* box. A dialog box appears with a list of sounds and a picture of a tape recorder. Select one of the sounds on the list. If you want to preview the sound, click *Play* on the tape recorder. Then click *OK* to get back to the *Actions* dialog box. Then click *Done.*

Adding Graphics to Cards

You can add graphics to cards by going to the *Objects* menu and selecting *Add a Graphic Object.* You will see a list of labels indicating the types of graphics that are available. Click on one of the labels. You will then see an arrangement of graphics associated with that label. Click on one of the selection tools at the top left-hand corner of the screen; this lets you ring the graphic you want. Then click *OK.* You will see the graphic on your card. Move the graphic to where you want it. Then click anywhere on the screen. A dialog box appears. The options in this box let you add sound and other special effects to your graphic.

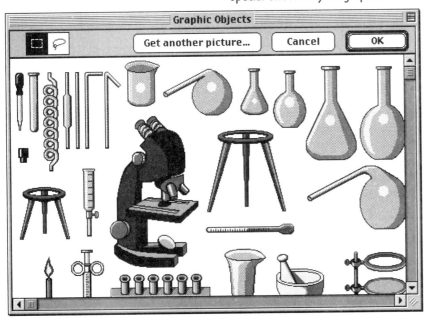

HyperStudio lets students experiment with text, graphics, sounds, and special effects to produce interesting presentations. Give students plenty of time to explore the program. As they play with the many fun features of *HyperStudio* and work through the activities in this book, they will become excited about creating colorful multimedia presentations on their own.

Keyboarding Skills

It is important that students learn basic keyboarding skills so that they can type quickly and accurately. To begin, show students which hand to use with which keys. The illustration below shows which keys are pressed with the left hand and which ones are pressed with the right. Enlarge the illustration and display it at your computer learning center as a reference for your students.

If you feel your students are ready for keyboarding, begin teaching them the proper finger placement. Have your students practice typing the letters located in the middle row (*a, s, d, f, g, h, j, k, l*) with the proper fingers; challenge them to type the letters without looking down at the keyboard. Later, let students practice typing letters in the top row and the bottom row. Eventually, have students type words and sentences without looking at the keyboard. Tell your students that as they increase their keyboarding skills, they will become more efficient in using the computer.

Note: There are many excellent software programs that teach typing skills.

You may wish to use portable keyboards in your classroom so that students can input stories without tying up the computer. Students type their stories into the portable keyboard. Afterwards, the story is downloaded into the computer for formatting and editing. These portable keyboards are available for both Macintosh and PC models. Schools could invest in a class set to be borrowed by teachers when their students need to process a large amount of text.

FS123297 Classroom Computer Center (5-6) © Copyright Frank Schaffer Publications, Inc.

Lesson Objective

The lessons on pages 12–15 are designed to give students guided practice with the *ClarisWorks* program. Each lesson focuses on specific tasks or tools. Students should follow the directions on the activity card. Because these are introductory lessons designed to give students practice and get them excited about using the software, it is not required that students print their work. If you would like students to print their work, you will need to give this specific direction since it does not appear on the activity cards.

Lesson Plan

1. Tell your students that they will be doing some basic lessons using *ClarisWorks*. Explain that the lessons will help them learn how to use the tools. Tell the students that the more practice they have with the tools, the more familiar they will become with *ClarisWorks* and the easier the activities will be.

2. Tell students that they double-click on the *ClarisWorks* icon in order to open the program. Then they select the *Word Processing* or *Painting* option (the lesson will specify which one will be used).

3. Explain that some of the paint lessons will require them to use certain tools from the tool palette. Go through each tool so students know what each one is called. Explain that in order to use a tool, students must click on the tool and then click on the screen.

4. Show students the activity cards. Explain that they are to follow the directions step by step. Let the students know that if they would like to experiment with the tools by doing more than what is directed on the activity card, they are free to do so.

5. Go over the directions of each card to ensure that students understand the instructions clearly. Then leave the cards at the computer learning center for students to work with independently.

6. Review procedures for quitting or exiting *ClarisWorks*. Remind students that they need to click on the *File* menu and select *Quit* or *Exit*.

Typing Text

1. Open the *ClarisWorks* program. Select the *Word Processing* option.

2. Type the following words:

   country

   city

   ocean

3. Use the delete or backspace key to delete the word *country*.

4. Type the following sentence. Use the shift key to make a capital letter.

   I found a map of Europe in an atlas.

5. Use the delete or backspace key to delete the word *Europe*.

6. Type a new word or phrase so that the sentence states something else that you can find in an atlas. Here is one example:

   I found a map of the United States in an atlas.

7. Practice typing another sentence on your own.

8. Quit or exit the program.

FS123297 Classroom Computer Center (5-6) © Copyright Frank Schaffer Publications, Inc.

reproducible

Text Tool Practice

1. Open the *ClarisWorks* program. Select the *Painting* option.

2. Select the text tool. Click on the screen.

3. Type the following words:

   baseball

   soccer

   basketball

4. Use the delete or backspace key to delete the word *baseball*.

5. Type the following sentence. Use the shift key to make a capital letter.

   I played baseball on Saturday.

6. Use the delete or backspace key to delete the words *played baseball*.

7. Type a new word or phrase so that the sentence states something else that you did on Saturday. Here is one example:

   I went hiking on Saturday.

8. Practice typing another sentence on your own.

9. Quit or exit the program.

reproducible

Pencil, Eraser, Shape, and Line Tools Practice

1. Open the *ClarisWorks* program. Select the *Painting* option.

2. Select the pencil tool.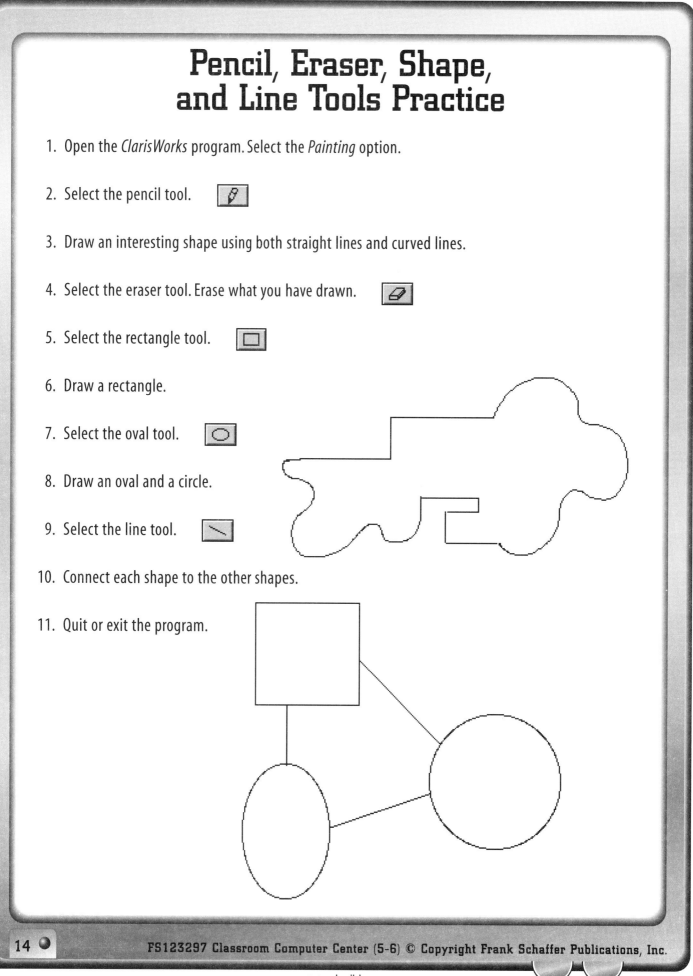

3. Draw an interesting shape using both straight lines and curved lines.

4. Select the eraser tool. Erase what you have drawn.

5. Select the rectangle tool.

6. Draw a rectangle.

7. Select the oval tool.

8. Draw an oval and a circle.

9. Select the line tool.

10. Connect each shape to the other shapes.

11. Quit or exit the program.

FS123297 Classroom Computer Center (5-6) © Copyright Frank Schaffer Publications, Inc.

reproducible

Paint Can, Spray Can, & Undo Practice

1. Open the *ClarisWorks* program. Select the *Painting* option.

2. Select the pencil tool. 🖊

   Draw a circle, but stop drawing just before the lines connect.

3. Select the paint can tool. 🪣

   Paint the circle. Remember that it is the tip of the paint can that pours the paint.

4. Look at the screen. The whole page got painted because the circle was not completely closed!

5. Click on the *Edit* menu at the top of the screen. Select *Undo Paint*. The color disappears!

6. Select the pencil tool. Close your circle. 🖊

7. Click on the paint can tool. Color your circle. 🪣

8. Click on the spray can tool. Choose a new color from the color palette. 🎨

9. Spray a background for your picture.

10. Quit or exit the program.

Lesson Objective

The lessons on pages 17–19 are designed to give students guided practice with *HyperStudio*. Each lesson focuses on basic functions of the program. Because these are introductory lessons designed to give students practice (and get them excited about using the software), they are not asked to print their work. If you would like students to print their work, you will need to give this specific direction since it does not appear on the activity cards.

HyperStudio 3.1

Lesson Plan

1. Explain to students that they will be doing some basic lessons using *HyperStudio*. These lessons will help them become accustomed to the tools and basic operations. Tell students that the more practice they have with the tools, the more familiar they will become with *HyperStudio* and the easier the activities will be.

2. Tell students that they double-click on the *HyperStudio* icon in order to open the program. Then they click on *New Stack*.

3. Tell students that one of the lessons will require them to use certain tools from the tool palette. Discuss the function of each tool with the class. Explain that in order to use a tool, students must click on the tool and then click on the screen.

4. Tell students that they will also be adding text objects (boxes that contain text), buttons, and graphics. Demonstrate the procedures first so that students can become familiar with these items.

5. Show students the activity cards. Explain that they are to follow the directions step by step. Let the students know that if they would like to experiment with the tools by doing more than what is directed on the activity card, they are free to do so.

6. Go over the directions of each card to ensure that students understand the instructions clearly. Then leave the cards at the computer learning center for students to work with independently.

7. Review procedures for quitting or exiting *HyperStudio*. Remind students that they need to click on the *File* menu and select *Quit HyperStudio* or *Exit HyperStudio*.

 FS123297 Classroom Computer Center (5-6) © Copyright Frank Schaffer Publications, Inc.

Text Object Lesson

1. Open the *HyperStudio* program. Select *New Stack* to begin a new card.

2. Add a text object (a box for typing in text). Do this by clicking on the *Objects* menu and selecting *Add a Text Object*. A box will appear on the card.

3. To move the box, click on it and drag it into place.

4. Click anywhere on the screen. A dialog box with several options will appear.

5. You will see a highlighted box that is labeled *Name*. For this lesson, you will not need to type anything in the box.

6. Pick a color for your text by clicking on the color box labeled *Text*. Pick a color for the background of the box by clicking on the color box labeled *Background*.

7. Click on *Style* to format your text. Another dialog box will appear. This box lets you choose the font, size, style, and alignment of your text.

8. Select *Helvetica* for the font, *18-point* for the size, *bold* for the style, and *center* for the alignment. Click *OK* when you are finished.

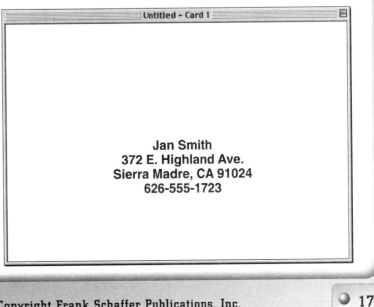

9. Type your name, address, and phone number.

10. Quit or exit the program.

Button Lesson

1. Open the *HyperStudio* program. Click on *New Stack* to see your new card.

2. Add a button to your card. Do this by clicking on the *Objects* menu and selecting *Add a Button*. A dialog box will appear.

3. Choose a shape for the button. Then type in a name (a label) for the button, such as *Click Here*.

4. Add a graphic (a picture) to the button. Do this by clicking on the *Show Icon* box. Graphics will appear. Click on the one you want. Then click *OK*. You will go back to the previous dialog box.

5. Choose the color of the text by clicking on the color box labeled *Name*. Choose the color of the button's background by clicking on the color box labeled *Background*. Then click *OK*. Your button will appear on the card.

6. Move the button where you want it by clicking on it and dragging it. Then click anywhere on the screen to add actions to your button. Actions include sounds and special effects.

7. A dialog box will appear with boxes labeled *Places to Go* and *Things to Do*. In the *Places to Go* box, click on *Next card*. A box labeled *Transitions* will appear. Choose a transition. Then click *OK* to return to the previous dialog box.

8. Click on *Play a Sound* in the *Things to Do* box to add a sound to your button. A choice of sounds will appear. Choose one sound. If you want to hear the sound, click on *Play*. When you are finished, click *OK* to return to the previous dialog box. Then click *Done*.

9. You will see your button on your card. Click on the *Tools* menu and select the hand tool. Then click on your button. See what happens!

10. Quit or exit the program.

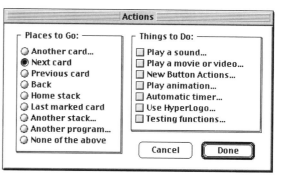

Graphics & Paint Tools Lesson

1. Open the *HyperStudio* program. Click on *New Stack* to see your new card.

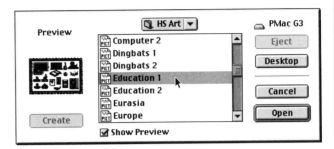

2. Click on the *Objects* menu and select *Add a Graphic Object*. Select *Open*. Graphic files will appear, along with a preview box. Select *Education*.

3. A selection of graphics will appear. Use the square-shaped tool located at the top left-hand corner to select the picture you want. Then click *OK*. The graphic will appear on your card.

4. Move the graphic where you want it. Then click anywhere on the screen. A dialog box will appear. (This box contains options for adding sound and other special effects to your graphic, but you won't be adding those elements in this lesson.) Click *OK*.

5. Select the paint can from the *Tools* menu at the top of the screen. If you like, click on the *Color* menu and change the color of the paint can. Then add color to the background of your card.

6. Use the other paint tools in the *Tools* menu to decorate your card. To change the colors of the paint tools, click on the *Color* menu.

7. Select the text tool and type your name. Then click anywhere on the screen. See if you can go back to your name and change a letter. You can't. It is important to remember that when you use the text tool to "paint" text on your card, the text can't be changed.

8. Quit or exit the program.

Software: *ClarisWorks* Word Processing Application (Apple)

Technology Prerequisites: Students must be able to highlight and format text and to use the spell check feature.

Content Skills: reading comprehension, creative writing, spelling

Technology Skills: keyboarding, formatting text, highlighting text, spell check

Literature: *The Paper Bag Princess* by Robert N. Munsch (Firefly Books Ltd., 1986), *The Frog Prince Continued* by Jon Scieszka (Viking, 1991), *The True Story of the 3 Little Pigs!* by Jon Scieszka (Viking, 1989)

Lesson Objective

In this creative writing lesson, students rewrite a familiar fairy tale by adding an unusual "twist" to the plot. The literature books suggested above are good examples to show your class.

Lesson Plan

1. Read any of the books listed above, or read another of your choice. Discuss how the author changed the original story line to create a humorous tale.

2. Tell students that they will write a fairy tale with an unusual "twist." Begin by brainstorming a list of fairy tales on the chalkboard. Then have each student choose one to rewrite.

3. Let students write their fairy tales at their desks before having them work on the computer. Have them add interesting titles to their stories. Tell them that they will be using the *Word Processing* feature in *ClarisWorks* to type their work. Add that they will format their text by choosing particular fonts, sizes, and styles. Remind them that they will need to use the *Font*, *Size*, and *Style* menus to format text.

4. Tell students to spell check their stories. To access the spell check feature, students will need to click on the *Edit*

menu. They will then select *Writing Tools* and click on *Check Document Spelling*.

5. Remind students to type their names at the bottom of the page before printing their work.

6. Remind students to quit or exit the program when they are finished so that the computer is ready for the next student.

Assessment Criteria

The student wrote an interesting fairy tale.

The student spelled all words correctly.

The student formatted the text correctly.

Fairy Tale With a Twist

1. Open the *ClarisWorks* program. Select the *Word Processing* option.

2. Type the title of your story.

3. Make the title bold. To do this, highlight the title. Then click on the *Style* menu and choose *Bold*.

4. Change the size of the title to 24-point by using the *Size* menu.

5. Change the font to any one you wish by using the *Font* menu.

6. Select the kind of text you want to use for your story. Use the *Style*, *Size*, and *Font* menus and click on the options you want.

7. Type your story.

8. Spell check your document. Click on the *Edit* menu. Select *Writing Tools*. Then select *Check Document Spelling*. Correct any spelling errors.

9. Type your name at the bottom of the page.

10. Print.

11. Quit or exit the program.

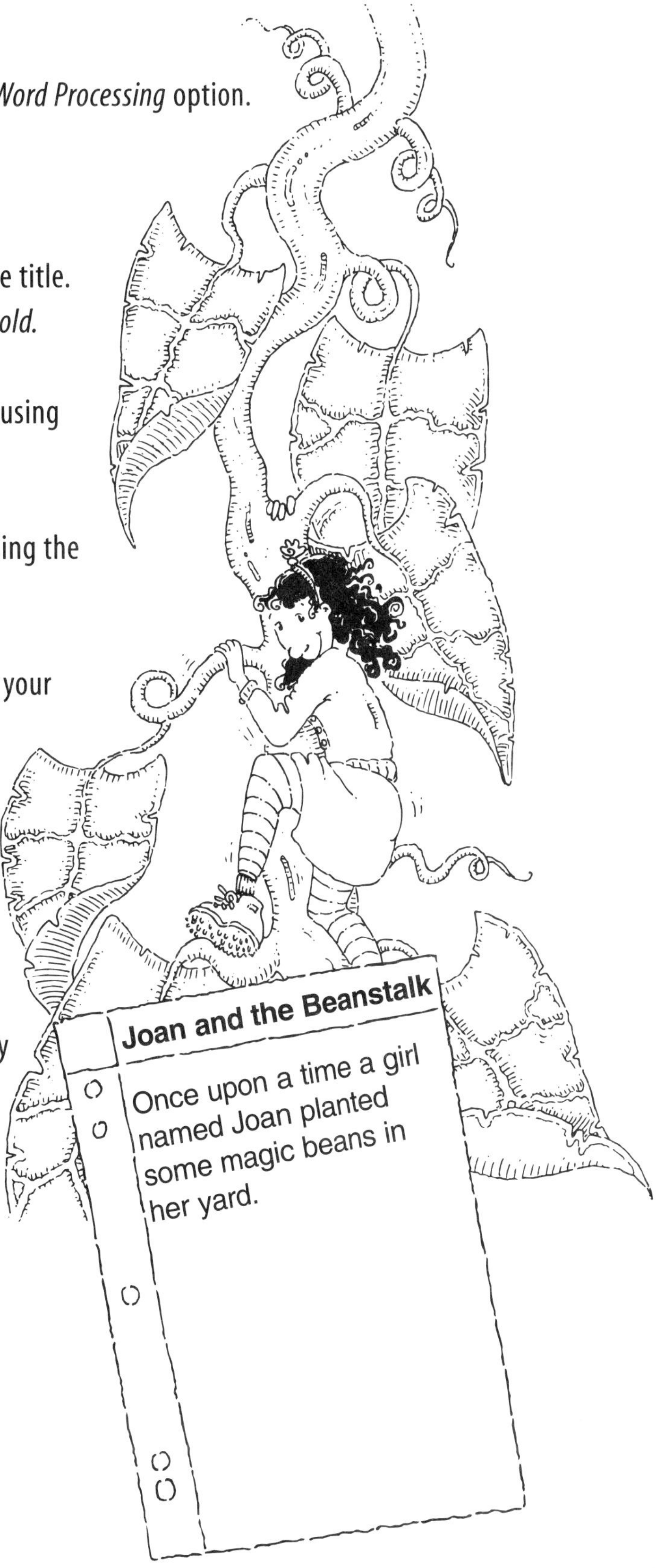

Joan and the Beanstalk

Once upon a time a girl named Joan planted some magic beans in her yard.

reproducible

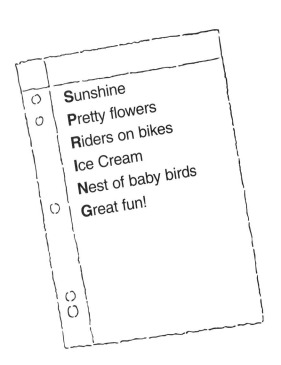

Sunshine
Pretty flowers
Riders on bikes
Ice Cream
Nest of baby birds
Great fun!

Software: *ClarisWorks* Word Processing Application (Apple)

Technology Prerequisites: Students must be able to highlight and format text. Students must also be able to use the spell check feature.

Content Skills: creative writing, poetry, spelling

Technology Skills: formatting text, highlighting text, spell check

Lesson Objective

This lesson introduces students to acrostic poems and gives practice in typing and formatting text. If you like, use this lesson as a supplement to a unit on poetry.

Lesson Plan

1. Write the poem shown above on the chalkboard. Read the poem with the class. Then underline the first letter in each poem. Guide the class into seeing that those letters form the word *spring*. Tell students that this type of poem is called an acrostic poem.

2. Next, have the class make up an acrostic poem together. Begin by choosing a word and writing it vertically on the chalkboard. Then have the students suggest words or phrases for each line of the poem.

3. Have the students write acrostic poems of their own. Then tell them that they will be typing their work on the computer and formatting the text. Explain that they will be changing the size of the type and bold facing certain letters. Remind students that they will need to use the *Size* and *Style* menus to make those changes.

4. Tell students they will spell check their documents. Explain that they will need to click on the *Edit* menu, and choose *Writing Tools*, and then select *Check Document Spelling*.

5. Remind students to type their names at the bottom of the page before printing their work.

6. Remind students to quit or exit the program when they are finished so that the computer is ready for the next student.

Assessment Criteria

The student wrote an acrostic poem.

The student formatted the text correctly.

The student spelled all words correctly.

An Acrostic Poem

1. Open the *ClarisWorks* program. Select the *Word Processing* option.

2. Type your acrostic poem.

3. Highlight the text of your poem. Click on the *Size* menu. Change the type size to 18-point.

4. Highlight the first letter of each line one at a time. Click on the *Style* menu and select *Bold*. Then click on the *Size* menu and change the letter to 24-point.

5. Spell check your document. To do this, click on the *Edit* menu and select *Writing Tools*. Click on *Check Document Spelling*. Correct any spelling errors.

6. Type your name at the bottom of the page.

7. Print.

8. Quit or exit the program.

Sunshine
Pretty flowers
Riders on bikes
Ice cream
Nest of baby birds
Great fun!

Software: *ClarisWorks* Word Processing Application (Apple)

Technology Prerequisites: Students must be able to insert a date and use the spell check feature.

Content Skills: writing a letter, spelling

Technology Skills: keyboarding, date insertion, spell check

Lesson Objective

Students will use the computer to type a letter to their "pen pals." They will use the spell check feature in *ClarisWorks* to help them proofread their work. Afterwards, the letters can be packaged and delivered.

Lesson Plan

1. Contact a teacher whose students are one grade below yours, and arrange to have your class write to them. Obtain a class list from that teacher and then pair up your students with the younger children. (Assign two students to one child if you have more students than the other teacher; assign one student to two children if you have less.) Tell students that they will be writing letters to their "pen pals" explaining what kinds of things the younger children can expect to learn in school next year.

2. Have students plan their letters at their desks first. They may just want to jot down some ideas about what they will say, or they may prefer to compose their entire letter.

3. When students are ready to work on the computer, have them enter the date at the top of the screen. To do this, they click on the *Edit* menu and select *Insert Date*; the date will then appear at the top left-hand corner.

4. Tell students that after they type their letters, they should read over their work carefully. Have them use the spell check feature to help them proofread their work. Tell students that they will need to go to the *Edit* menu, select *Writing Tools*, and then click on *Check Document Spelling*.

5. Remind students to type their names at the bottom of the page before printing their work.

6. Remind students to quit or exit the program when they are finished so that the computer is ready for the next student.

Assessment Criteria

The student wrote a complete letter.

The student proofread the letter.

The student inserted the date correctly.

The student spelled all words correctly.

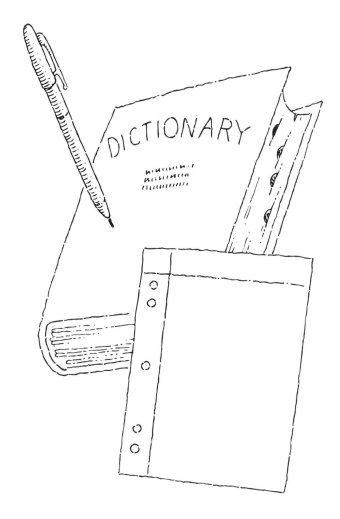

A "Pen Pal" Letter

1. Open the *ClarisWorks* program. Select the *Word Processing* option.

2. Insert the date at the top of your letter. Do this by clicking on the *Edit* menu and selecting *Insert Date*. The date will appear at the top of the letter.

3. Press the return key twice to drop down two lines from the date.

4. Type your letter.

5. Look over your letter carefully and proofread your work.

6. Spell check your document. To do this, click on the *Edit* menu, select *Writing Tools*, and *Check Document Spelling*. Correct any spelling errors.

7. Type your name at the bottom of the page.

8. Print.

9. Quit or exit the program.

May 3, 1999

Dear Megan,

Our class is learning a lot this year! Today we practiced how to type a letter on the computer. It was a lot of fun! It's much faster than writing a letter by hand. I hope I can show you how one day!

Take care!

Lynn

reproducible

Software: *ClarisWorks* Painting Application (Apple)

Technology Prerequisites: Students must be able to use the pencil tool, paintbrush, paint can, and spray can as well as change the colors of the paint tools using the color palette. Students must also be able to use the text tool, spell check, and thesaurus.

Content Skills: descriptive writing, spelling

Technology Skills: pencil tool, paintbrush, paint can, spray can, color palette, text tool, spell check, thesaurus

Lesson Objective

In this lesson, students will write and illustrate their own advertisements. They will also use word processing tools (spell check and thesaurus) within the paint application.

Lesson Plan

1. Show a variety of magazine ads to the class. Discuss these questions: *What are the ads trying to convey? To whom are they trying to appeal? What are some of the "hot" words used in the copy?* Ask the class to point out the descriptive words used in the ads. Discuss how the words help sell the product.

2. Invite students to write an ad for a real or imaginary product. They may pick a product of their own or write about one that you assign. Students will draw pictures for their ad with the paint tools. They will use the text tool to type the ad copy and then look up options for alternative words by using the thesaurus available in *ClarisWorks*. Afterwards, they will spell check their documents. Tell the class that both the thesaurus and spell check features are found in the *Edit* menu under *Writing Tools*.

3. Remind students to type their names at the bottom of the page before printing their work.

4. Remind students to quit or exit the program when they are finished so that the computer is ready for the next student.

Assessment Criteria

The student designed an interesting ad.

The student used descriptive words.

The student spelled all words correctly.

The student used the text tool and painting tools correctly.

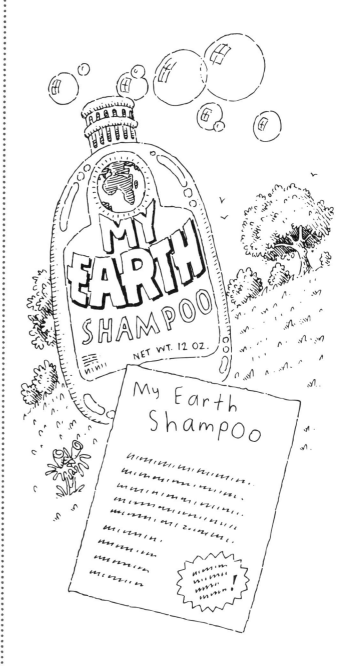

Create an Ad

1. Open the *ClarisWorks* program. Select the *Painting* option.

2. Use the paint tools to illustrate your advertisement. Use the color palette to change the colors of the paint tools.

3. Select the text tool and type your ad copy. Use interesting words to describe your product.

4. Look in the thesaurus for other words that might make better choices for some of the words you've used. To do this, highlight the word that you might replace. Then click on the

Word Finder® Thesaurus
Find: [   ] Lookup   Last Word   Cancel   Replace

   Edit menu, select *Writing Tools*, and click on *Thesaurus*. You will see a list of words. If you see one you like, click on it and select *Replace*. You will get back to your document, and the new word will appear in place of the one you highlighted.

5. Spell check your document. To do this, click on the *Edit* menu, select *Writing Tools*, and then click on *Check Document Spelling*. Correct any spelling errors.

6. Type your name at the bottom of the page.

7. Print.

8. Quit or exit the program.

MY EARTH SHAMPOO

This all-natural shampoo uses only the finest herbs. It will make your hair shinier, silkier, and healthier than it has ever been!

reproducible

Software: *ClarisWorks* Word Processing Application (Apple)

Technology Prerequisites: Students must be able to use the spell check and thesaurus.

Content Skills: writing a business letter, spelling, synonyms

Technology Skills: keyboarding, spell check, thesaurus

Lesson Objective

In this lesson, students will compose a business letter discussing a topic of interest.

Lesson Plan

1. Get the addresses of local museums, zoos, organizations, and other places that students might wish to contact. Then tell students that they will practice writing business letters that request information about a particular topic. For example, they could write to a museum for details about a current display or ask an organization for a pamphlet outlining its goals and services. Students may also look in the Yellow Pages for suggestions on what places to contact.

2. Discuss with your class what a business letter looks like. Tell students that the sender's address appears at the top left-hand side of the page. The date and the company's name and address appears below that, followed by the greeting, the body of the letter, the closing, and the signature.

3. Have students compose a rough draft of their letters at their desks before going to the computer. Remind the class that the letters should be brief, clear, and concise.

4. Tell students that after they type their letters, they should use the thesaurus and spell check features to edit their work. To access these features, students will need to click on the *Edit* menu, select *Writing Tools*, and click on *Check Document Spelling* or *Thesaurus*.

5. Remind students to quit or exit the program when they are finished so that the computer is ready for the next student.

Assessment Criteria

The student wrote the business letter using the proper format.

The student proofread and edited the letter.

The student spelled all words correctly.

The student used the thesaurus.

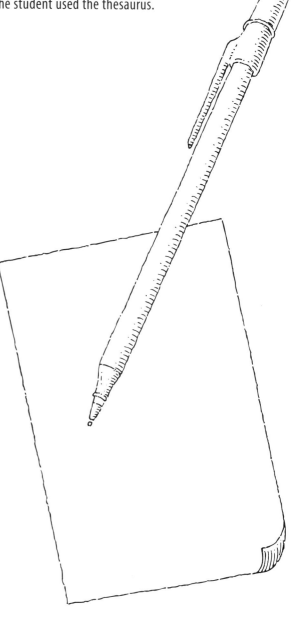

 FS123297 Classroom Computer Center (5-6) © Copyright Frank Schaffer Publications, Inc.

A Business Letter

1. Open the *ClarisWorks* program. Select the *Word Processing* option.

2. Type your business letter. Look at the sample below for the proper format.

3. Proofread your letter. Check to see that you used capitals and punctuation properly. Read each sentence to make sure that it makes sense.

4. Look in the thesaurus for other words that might make your letter clearer or more interesting. To do this, highlight a word that you want to replace. Then click on the *Edit* menu, select *Writing Tools*, and click on *Thesaurus*. You will see a list of words. If you see one you like, click on it and select *Replace*.

5. Spell check your document. To do this, click on the *Edit* menu, select *Writing Tools*, and then click on *Check Document Spelling*. Correct any spelling errors.

6. Print.

7. Quit or exit the program.

634 Maple Ave.
Anyville, CA 90000

August 5, 1999

Sea Magic Aquarium
401 Oceanview Avenue
Anyville, CA 90000

Dear Sir or Madam,

I would like to take 10 people to the aquarium this month. Do you have a special rate for groups? Also, can you tell me how long your exhibit on prehistoric sea life will be on display? I am enclosing a self-addressed, stamped envelope for your reply. Thank you.

Yours truly,

Alina Briggs

Software: *ClarisWorks* Word Processing Application (Apple)

Technology Prerequisites: Students must be able to type a report, format text, and use spell check.

Content Skills: writing, spelling

Technology Skills: keyboarding, formatting text, saving files, using spell check

Lesson Objective

This lesson will let students create news articles about school happenings. Later, they will format their work so that the articles contain features similar to those in a newsletter.

Lesson Plan

1. Show your class a sample of a newsletter. Point out these features of a newsletter: the header (title) at the top of the page, the footer at the bottom of the page, columns (two or more), and individual articles. Tell your students that they will be reporting on school happenings and using the computer to format their work to look like a newsletter.

2. Brainstorm with the class the kinds of school news students might report on. Suggestions could include school events, current topics of study, classroom happenings, and interviews of students and school staff. Then give the students ample time to write their articles. Once a students has composed a rough draft, let him or her type the report on the computer. Tell the students that their work should fill about 3/4 of a page.

3. When students have finished typing their articles, have them spell check their work. To do this, they must click on the *Edit* menu, select *Writing Tools*, and click on *Check Document Spelling*.

4. Have each student save his or her work as *story.their initials*. Tell students that they will retrieve their files later and format their reports to look more like a newsletter article.

5. Remind students to quit or exit the program when they are finished so that the computer is ready for the next student.

Assessment Criteria

The student wrote an interesting article.

The student spelled all words correctly.

The student saved his or her file correctly.

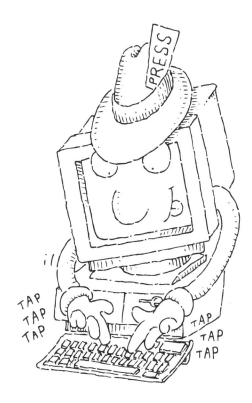

School News—Part 1

1. Open the *ClarisWorks* program. Select the *Word Processing* option.

2. Type an interesting article about school. The article may be about a classroom or school happening. Or, the article may tell about an interview with a student or staff member at the school.

3. After you finish typing, look over your story. Your work should fill about 3/4 of the page. Proofread your article. Check that you used capitals and punctuation correctly. Read over your work to make sure that each sentence makes sense.

3. Spell check your document. To do this, click on the *Edit* menu, select *Writing Tools*, and click on *Check Document Spelling*.

4. Type your name at the end of the article.

5. Save your article. To do this, click on the *File* menu and select *Save*. Save the file as **story.your initials**.

6. Quit or exit the program.

Software: *ClarisWorks* Word Processing Application (Apple)

Technology Prerequisites: Students must be able to use the menus to insert columns, headers, and footers. They must also be able to retrieve files and copy, paste, and format text.

Content Skill: writing

Technology Skills: keyboarding, inserting headers and footers, inserting columns, copying, pasting, formatting text, saving and retrieving files

Lesson Objective

This lesson will let students format their articles to make them resemble newsletters. If you like, students can later use the experience they gain in this lesson to create a class newsletter.

Lesson Plan

1. Tell students that they will be formatting the articles they wrote earlier. Explain that they will be creating a header and footer for their pages. They will also be dividing their page into two columns.

2. Tell students that they will open a new document and add a header and footer. To add a header, they will click on the *Format* menu, select *Insert Header*, and type the name of their article. To add a footer, they will click on the *Format* menu, select *Insert Footer*, and type the name of their school and its address and phone number. They will also divide the page into two columns by clicking on the two-column icon in the tool bar.

3. Once the page is formatted, students will retrieve their articles. They will click on the *File* menu and select *Open*. Then they will click on the file they saved. That article will then appear on the screen.

4. Students will copy the article by clicking on the *Edit* menu, choosing *Select All*, and selecting *Copy*. They will close the current document by clicking on the *File* menu and selecting *Close*. They will then paste the text into their formatted document by clicking on the *Edit* menu and selecting *Paste*.

5. Tell students to save their formatted document as *news.their initials*.

6. Remind students to quit or exit the program when they are finished so that the computer is ready for the next student.

Assessment Criteria

The student formatted the header and footer correctly.

The student formatted the columns correctly.

The student copied and pasted text correctly.

School News–Part 2

1. Open the *ClarisWorks* program. Select the *Word Processing* option.

2. Add a header. The header will be the title of your article. To add a header, click on the *Edit* menu and select *Insert Header*. Type the title.

3. Change the size of the type to 24-point by clicking on the *Size* menu.

4. Add a footer. Do this by clicking on the *Edit* menu and selecting *Insert Footer*. Type your school's name, address, and phone number. The footer will appear at the bottom of your page.

5. Divide the page into two columns by clicking on the column button that shows two bars. This button is located in the tool bar at the top of the page.

6. Add the article that you wrote earlier. To do this, click on the *File* menu and select *Open*. A list of file names will appear. Find the one you want and then click on *Open*.

7. Your article will appear. Copy it by clicking on the *Edit* menu. Choose *Select All* and then *Copy*. Close the file by clicking on the *File* menu and selecting *Close*.

8. You will be back in your original document. Paste your article by clicking on the *Edit* menu and selecting *Paste*. Your article will appear, formatted in two columns.

9. Save your file. Click on the *File* menu and select *Save*. Save the article as **news.your initials**.

10. Print.

11. Quit or exit the program.

reproducible

Software: *HyperStudio* (Roger Wagner Publishing)

Technology Prerequisites: Students must be able to use the text tool and pencil tool. They must also be able to use the paint tools and change their colors with the color palette. Students must be able to create new cards and text objects; they will need to know how to add buttons and transitions.

Content Skills: writing, descriptive language, summarizing

Technology Skills: text tool, pencil tool, paint tools (paintbrush, paint can), color palette, cards, text objects, buttons (including button sounds and text), transitions, special effects

Lesson Objective

In this lesson, students will create a book report using graphics, sounds, and special effects. If you have a large screen projection device (see page 2), you can let students present their multimedia reports to the class.

Lesson Plan

1. Tell students that they will be using *HyperStudio* to create interesting book reports. Students will need to make five cards for their stack: title card, setting card, characters card, summary card, and critique card.

2. Tell students that their first card will be the title card. The title card should include the book's title and author as well as an interesting picture that shows what the story is about. The class will need to use the text tool, pencil tool, and paint tools to create their card. Remind students that they can change the thickness of the pencil line and paintbrush strokes by clicking on the *Options* menu and selecting *Line Size* or *Brush Shape*.

3. When students have finished making their first card, they will add a button to it. The button will let them move from the first card to the second card. To add a button, they will click on the *Objects* menu and select *Add a Button*. A dialog box will appear. Students will need to choose a shape for the button and type its name (the words that appear on the button). They will also choose the color of the button's name and the color of the background. After students click *OK*, they will see the button on their card.

4. Once the button appears on their card, students will move it into place by clicking on it and dragging it. Then they will click anywhere on the screen to add actions to the button. (Actions are sounds and special effects.) A dialog box with two boxes labeled *Places to Go* and *Play a Sound* will appear. In the *Places to Go* box, students will select *Next card*. Another dialog box will appear, and students will choose a transition (a special effect that takes place when there is movement from one card to the next). When *OK* is clicked, students will return to the previous dialog box.

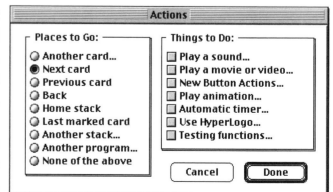

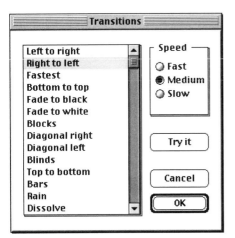

5. Students will click on *Play a Sound* to choose a sound for their button. A dialog box will appear, and students will make their sound selection and click *OK* to return to the previous dialog box. When they click on *Done*, they will see their card and the button they created.

6. To add a second card to their stack, students will click on the *Edit* menu and select *New card*. On the second card, students will need to add a text object (a box that encloses text) by clicking on the *Objects* menu and selecting *Add a Text Object*. A box will appear on the card. To move it, students will click on it and drag it in place. Then they will click anywhere on the screen to format the text. A dialog box will appear.

7. Since students will not be naming the text object, they will not type anything in the highlighted *Name* box. They will click on the color boxes, however, to pick a color for the text and for the background. Then they will click on *Style* in order to get a dialog box that gives options for *font*, *style*, *size*, and *alignment* of text. Once students select their options and click *OK*, they can begin typing the text. (The second card should give information about the story setting.)

8. When students have completed typing the text for their second card, they will use the paint tools to decorate the card. Students will then follow the procedure described in steps 3–5 to add a button to their second card.

9. Students will follow the procedure described in the steps above to add the rest of the cards to their stack. The third card should list the main characters of the story. The card can be decorated with a picture of at least one of the characters. The fourth card should give a summary of the book. The fifth card should tell whether the students would recommend the book and why or why not.

10. When adding the button for the fifth card, students will need to indicate that the movement should be from the fifth card to the first card, not the next card. To do this, students will need to select *Another card* instead of *Next card* when choosing *Places to Go*. A dialog box with arrows will appear. Students will use the arrows to find the first card in the stack and then click *OK*. This will "loop" the stack. Have students test their stacks by clicking on *Move* and selecting *First Card*. Then then can check their entire presentation by making sure each button works correctly.

11. When students have completed their book report, they should save the file as *report.their initials*.

12. Remind students to quit or exit the program when they are finished. If you have a large screen projection device (see page 2), let students present their brochures to the class.

Assessment Criteria

The student presented accurate information about a book.

The student wrote a thoughtful critique of the book.

The student created the cards correctly.

The student looped the cards correctly.

The student added buttons correctly.

Multimedia Book Report

1. Open the *HyperStudio* program. Select *New Stack*.

2. You will see your first card. This will be your title card. Use the text tool to type the title and author of the book. Include your name on the card. Use the paint tools to draw a picture that represents the book you read.

3. Add a button to the card. Click on the *Objects* menu and select *Add a Button*. A dialog box will appear.

4. Choose a shape for the button. Then type a name for the button. (The name is the word or phrase that you want to see on the button.)

5. Click on the color boxes and choose a color for the name and for the background. Click *OK*.

6. The button will appear on the first card. Move it by clicking on it and dragging it into place. Then click anywhere on the screen. A dialog box labeled *Actions* will appear. It lets you choose actions for your button.

7. In the *Places to Go* box, select *Next card*. You will then see a dialog box labeled *Transitions*. A transition is a special effect that takes place when you move from one card to another. Choose a transition and then click *OK*. You will get back to the dialog box labeled *Actions*.

8. Click on *Play a Sound* in the *Things to Do* box. Then choose a sound for your button. If you want to hear the sound, click on *Play*. When you are finished, click *OK* to get back to the *Actions* dialog box. Then click *Done* to get back to the first card.

9. Add a new card by clicking on the *Edit* menu and selecting *New card*. Your second card will appear on the screen.

10. Add a text object by clicking on the *Objects* menu and selecting *Add a Text Object*. A box will appear. You will use this box to hold your text. To move the box, click on it and drag it into place. Click anywhere on the screen. A dialog box labeled *Text Appearance* will appear.

FS123297 Classroom Computer Center (5-6) © Copyright Frank Schaffer Publications, Inc.

reproducible

Multimedia Book Report

11. Do not type anything in the *Name* box. However, pick a color for the text and for the background of the box.

12. Click on *Style*. You will see a dialog box with options for font, style, size, and alignment of text. Make your selections and then click *OK*. You will get back to the previous dialog box. Click *OK* to return to your card.

13. Your second card will give information about the setting of the story. Type the text. Then use the paint tools to decorate the card. Repeat steps 3–8 to add a button to your second card.

14. Repeat steps 9–12 to add a third card. The third card should list the main characters of the story. Use the text object to type the list and then use the paint tools to decorate the card. Repeat steps 3–8 to add a button to your third card.

15. Repeat step 14 to add a fourth card and a button for it. The fourth card should give a summary of the book. Type in the text and decorate the card.

16. Repeat steps 9–12 to add a fifth card. This card should tell whether or not you would recommend the book and why. Type in the text and decorate the card. Then add a button by repeating steps 3–8, but choose the sound before the transition. Then select *Another card* instead of *Next card* for *Places to Go*. A dialog box with arrows will appear. Click on the arrows until you get to the first card in your stack. When you reach this card, click *OK*. This will "loop" the cards in the stack.

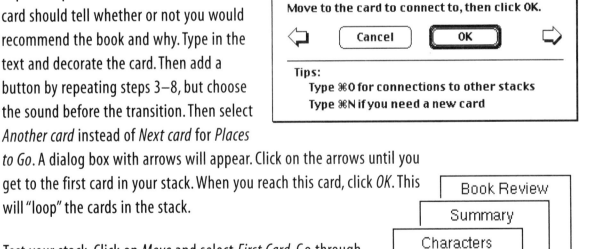

17. Test your stack. Click on *Move* and select *First Card*. Go through your stack and check that each button works correctly.

18. Save the file as **report.yourinitials**.

19. Quit or exit the program.

reproducible

Software: *ClarisWorks* Painting Application (Apple)

Technology Prerequisites: Students must be able to use the rectangle tool, text tool, and line tool.

Content Skills: geometry, critical thinking

Technology Skills: line tool, rectangle tool, text tool

Literature: *Grandfather Tang's Story* by Ann Tompert (Crown, 1990)

Lesson Objective

In this lesson, students will use the computer to make tangram shapes. After they print the shapes, they will cut them out and use them to make make a variety of pictures.

Lesson Plan

1. Read *Grandfather Tang's Story* to your class. Afterwards, tell the class that the pictures in the story were made from tangram shapes. Explain that a tangram is a Chinese puzzle that is made up of seven geometric shapes—a square, five triangles, and a rhomboid. The shapes can be pieced together to make many kinds of pictures. Tell students that they will be making their own tangram shapes with the computer.

2. Tell students that they will need to draw a large square using the rectangle tool in *ClarisWorks*. They should make the square big enough to cover the entire computer screen.

3. Tell students that after they have drawn the square, they should follow the tangram drawing on the activity sheet to draw the lines within the square. They should use the line tool to draw the lines.

4. Remind students to use the text tool to type their names at the bottom of the page before printing their work.

5. Remind students to quit or exit the program when they are finished so that the computer is ready for the next student.

6. Have the students glue their shapes onto heavy paper. After they cut out the shapes, have them write their names on the back of each piece of their tangram. Then give them time to explore their tangrams.

Assessment Criteria

The student drew the tangram correctly.

The student used the rectangle tool, line tool, and text tool correctly.

The student arranged the tangram shapes to make interesting pictures.

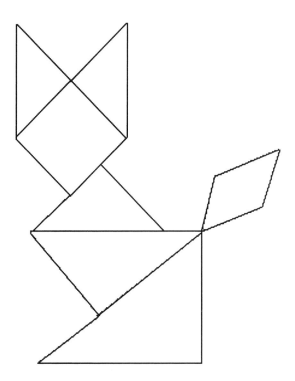

Tangram Challenge

1. Open the *ClarisWorks* program. Select the *Painting* option.

2. Select the rectangle tool. Draw a square large enough to fill most of the screen.

3. Select the line tool. Draw lines in the square to match the picture on the right. When you are done, you will have made a Chinese puzzle called a tangram.

4. Select the text tool and type your name at the bottom of the page.

5. Print.

6. Quit or exit the program.

7. Glue your tangram onto heavy paper. Cut out the shapes. Write your name on the back of each piece. Use the shapes to make interesting pictures.

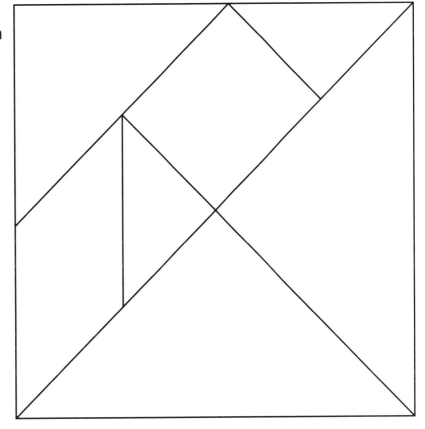

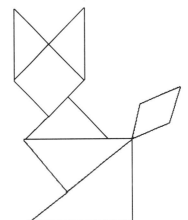

reproducible

Roman Numerals

Software: *ClarisWorks* Painting Application (Apple)

Technology Prerequisites: Students must be able to use the text tool.

Content Skills: Roman numerals, addition, subtraction

Technology Skills: keyboarding, shift key

Lesson Objective

In this lesson, students will learn to read and write Roman numerals.

Lesson Plan

1. Tell your class that the ancient Romans invented Roman numerals and that we still use Roman numerals today. Name some examples of items that display numerals. (Examples may include clocks, page numbers or chapter numbers in books, and copyright dates.) Then introduce these Roman numerals to the class:

1 = I	5 = V	10 = X	50 = L
100 = C	500 = D	1000 = M	

2. Have students practice reading and writing Roman numerals. Explain that Roman numerals are combined to form new numbers. For example, CLX means 160 (100 + 50 + 10). Generally, a smaller numeral appearing before a larger numeral indicates that the smaller amount is subtracted from the larger one. For example, IV means 4 and IX means 9.

3. Give students practice in writing Roman numerals for Arabic numerals and vice versa. Then reinforce the activity with the computer. Let students follow the directions on the accompanying activity card to type both Roman numerals and Arabic numerals. Remind the class to use the shift key to make the capital letters.

4. Remind students to type their names at the bottom of the page before printing their work.

5. Remind students to quit or exit the program when they are finished so that the computer is ready for the next student.

Assessment Criteria

The student identified the Roman numerals correctly.

The student typed the Roman numerals correctly.

The student used the shift key correctly.

FS123297 Classroom Computer Center (5-6) © Copyright Frank Schaffer Publications, Inc.

Roman Numerals

1. Open the *ClarisWorks* program. Select the *Word Processing* option.

2. Type the Roman numerals below. Beside each one, type the matching number. Use the chart to help you.

   XXV _____

   CXIII _____

   CCLI _____

3. Type the following problems. Type the answers in Roman numerals.

   XX + XVI = _____

   VII + XXIV = _____

   C – XXV = _____

   DCC – LIV = _____

4. Type the numbers below. Type the matching Roman numerals.

   858 _____

   1348 _____

5. Type your name at the bottom of the page.

6. Print.

7. Quit or exit the program.

Spreadsheet Practice

Software: *ClarisWorks* Painting Application (Apple)

Technology Prerequisites: Students must be familiar with parts of a spreadsheet (header, cell, column, row).

Content Skill: multiplication

Technology Skills: identifying parts of a spreadsheet, entering formulas

Lesson Objective

In this lesson, students will learn how to enter multiplication formulas on spreadsheets.

Lesson Plan

1. Write *42 x 36 =* and ask students how they could find the answer. (Examples: paper and pencil, calculator) Then tell students that they will be learning how spreadsheets are useful for solving math problems.

2. Tell students that they will be using the spreadsheet option in *ClarisWorks*. Remind them that they will need to double-click on the *ClarisWorks* icon and select *Spreadsheet*. Then go through the following procedure with the class. If you have a large screen projection device (page 2), demonstrate the steps described below.

3. Tell students to create a header by clicking on the *Format* menu and selecting *Insert Header*. Have each student type *Math Problems* and his or her name for this lesson.

4. Point out the rows and columns. The rows are numbered at the left and the columns are labeled with letters at the top. Point out the cells; explain that they are named by the column and row in which they appear. For example, A1 appears in Column A and in Row 1. Point out the menus and the entry bar at the top of the screen. Explain that to enter data on the spreadsheet, students will click on the appropriate cell and start typing; what they type appears in the entry bar. When the checkmark is clicked, the data appears in the cell.

5. Have students enter numbers for Columns A and Column B. For Column C, they will enter formulas that let them multiply a number from Column A with one from Column B. They will start each formula with an equal sign, followed by a cell name, asterisk (the multiplication symbol) and cell name. For example, **=A1*B1** means that the number in A1 is to be multiplied by the number in B1. The answer will appear in Column C.

6. After students have done the multiplication problems on the activity card, they can experiment by solving other multiplication problems on the spreadsheet. Afterwards, let the students print their work.

7. Remind students to quit or exit the program when they are finished.

Assessment Criteria

The student entered the header correctly.

The student entered data in the appropriate cells.

The student entered multiplication formulas correctly.

	A	B	C	
1	1	3	3	
2	2	4	8	
3	3	5	15	
4	4	6	24	
5	5	7	35	
6				
7				

Spreadsheet Practice

1. Open the *ClarisWorks* program. Select the *Spreadsheet* option.

2. Insert a header. (A header is a title.) To do this, click on the *Format* menu and select *Insert Header*. Then type **Math Problems**. Hit the return key. Type your name on the second line.

3. You will use the spreadsheet to solve some multiplication problems. First click on cell A1 (Column A, Row 1) and type 1. Click on the checkmark at the top of the spreadsheet to see the 1 appear in the cell.

4. Click on cell B1 (Column B, Row 1) and type 3. Click on the checkmark to see the 3 appear in the cell.

5. Click on C1 (Column C, Row 1). Type **=A1*B1** (the formula for multiplying the number in A1 by the one in B1). Click on the checkmark. The number **3** (1 x 3) will appear in the cell.

6. Follow the procedure described in steps 3, 4, and 5. Type the following numbers and formulas in the cells:

   A2 – **2**   B2 – **4**   C2 – the formula for multiplying A2 by B2 **(=A2*B2)**

   A3 – **3**   B3 – **5**   C3 – the formula for multiplying A3 by B3

   A4 – **4**   B4 – **6**   C4 – the formula for multiplying A4 by B4

   A5 – **5**   B5 – **7**   C5 – the formula for multiplying A5 by B5

Each time you will see the answer to the multiplication problem appear in Column C.

7. Try changing the numbers in Columns A or B. Use one-digit, two-digit, and three-digit numbers. See what happens to the numbers in Column C.

8. When you have finished experimenting with the spreadsheet, print it.

9. Quit or exit the program.

reproducible

A Weighty Challenge

Software: *ClarisWorks* Spreadsheet Application (Apple)

Technology Prerequisites: Students must be able to enter spreadsheet formulas and insert headers.

Content Skills: multiplication, algebra, mass, gravity

Technology Skills: spreadsheet formulas, headers

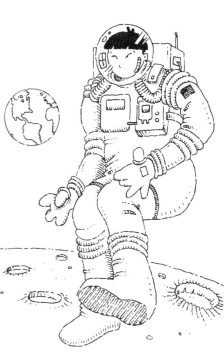

Lesson Objective

Students learn that the force of gravity is different on Earth than it is on the moon or the other planets, and that this difference affects the weight of an object. Students use the spreadsheet in *ClarisWorks* to chart how an object's weight varies, depending on its location in the solar system.

Lesson Plan

1. Show your students pictures of astronauts on the moon. Tell them that even though the astronauts had to wear heavy equipment, they were able to walk easily on the moon because they were not as heavy as they were on Earth. Explain that the force of gravity on the Earth is six times greater than on the moon; this means that the astronauts weighed only one-sixth of what they weighed on Earth. Explain that the force of gravity is weaker on the moon because the moon's mass (the amount of matter) is much smaller than Earth's.

2. Students create a spreadsheet to compare weights on Earth with weights on the moon and planets. They select the spreadsheet option in *ClarisWorks*.

3. Next, students insert the header by clicking on the *Format* menu and selecting *Insert Header*. They type *Weights in Outer Space* and then add their names on the second line.

4. Once students have created the header, they enter the names of the moon and planets in Column A, from A1 to A10. They enter 100 (weight in pounds) in Column B, from B1 to B10.

5. In Column C, students enter numbers that compare the force of gravity on the moon and the planets to that on Earth. For example, they will enter .17 for the moon, which means that if the force of gravity on Earth were represented by the number 1, then the force of gravity on the moon would be one-sixth of 1. The numbers to be keyed-in are listed on the activity card.

	A	B	C	D
1	Earth's Moon	100	0.17	
2	Mercury	100	0.38	
3	Venus	100	0.9	
4	Earth	100	1	
5	Mars	100	0.38	
6	Jupiter	100	2.87	
7	Saturn	100	1.32	
8	Uranus	100	0.93	
9	Neptune	100	1.23	
10	Pluto	100	0.06	

	A	B	C	D
1	Earth's Moon	100	0.17	17
2	Mercury	100	0.38	
3	Venus	100	0.9	
4	Earth	100	1	
5	Mars	100	0.38	
6	Jupiter	100	2.87	
7	Saturn	100	1.32	
8	Uranus	100	0.93	
9	Neptune	100	1.23	
10	Pluto	100	0.06	

	A	B	C	D
1	Earth's Moon	100	0.17	17
2	Mercury	100	0.38	38
3	Venus	100	0.9	90
4	Earth	100	1	100
5	Mars	100	0.38	38
6	Jupiter	100	2.87	287
7	Saturn	100	1.32	132
8	Uranus	100	0.93	93
9	Neptune	100	1.23	123
10	Pluto	100	0.06	6

	A	B	C	D
1	Earth's Moon	120	0.17	20.4
2	Mercury	120	0.38	45.6
3	Venus	120	0.9	108
4	Earth	120	1	120
5	Mars	120	0.38	45.6
6	Jupiter	120	2.87	344.4
7	Saturn	120	1.32	158.4
8	Uranus	120	0.93	111.6
9	Neptune	120	1.23	147.6
10	Pluto	120	0.06	7.2

6. In Column D, students enter the formulas for computing relative weights. In D1, they enter the formula for determining weight on the moon: =**B1*C1**. Once the formula is entered, the relative weight is automatically calculated in D1.

7. Students enter the appropriate formulas in the remaining cells in Column D. Once all the formulas have been entered, students will see that something weighing 100 pounds on Earth has varying weights in outer space.

8. Students print the spreadsheet. Then have them change the weight Column B to 120 to see that the spreadsheet automatically adjusts the weights in Column D.

9. Let the students experiment using other numbers for the weights. Ask them how much they would weigh on the moon or the other planets.

10. When students have finished experimenting, let them print their final spreadsheet.

11. Remind students to quit or exit the program when they are finished.

Assessment Criteria

The student entered data on the spreadsheet correctly.

The student entered the formulas correctly.

The student experimented with the weights.

A Weighty Challenge

1. Open the *ClarisWorks* program. Select the *Spreadsheet* option.

2. Insert the header. To do this, click on the *Format* menu and select *Insert Header*. Type **Comparing Weights**. Then hit the return key and type your name on the second line.

3. Enter the following names in Column A:

   Earth's Moon
   Mercury
   Venus
   Earth
   Mars
   Jupiter
   Saturn
   Uranus
   Neptune
   Pluto

	A	B	C	D
1	Earth's Moon			
2	Mercury			
3	Venus			
4	Earth			
5	Mars			
6	Jupiter			
7	Saturn			
8	Uranus			
9	Neptune			
10	Pluto			

4. Enter **100** in Column B for rows 1 to 10. The 100 represents a weight of 100 pounds.

5. Enter the following numbers in Column C. The numbers show how the moon and planets compare in mass to the Earth.

Earth's Moon	.17
Mercury	.38
Venus	.90
Earth	1.00
Mars	.38
Jupiter	2.87
Saturn	1.32
Uranus	.93
Neptune	1.23
Pluto	.06

	A	B	C	D
1	Earth's Moon	100	0.17	
2	Mercury	100	0.38	
3	Venus	100	0.9	
4	Earth	100	1	
5	Mars	100	0.38	
6	Jupiter	100	2.87	
7	Saturn	100	1.32	
8	Uranus	100	0.93	
9	Neptune	100	1.23	
10	Pluto	100	0.06	

A Weighty Challenge

6. Enter the formulas to find out how much a 100-pound weight would weigh on the moon and the planets. First enter the formula for the moon. Click on D1. Type the following formula:

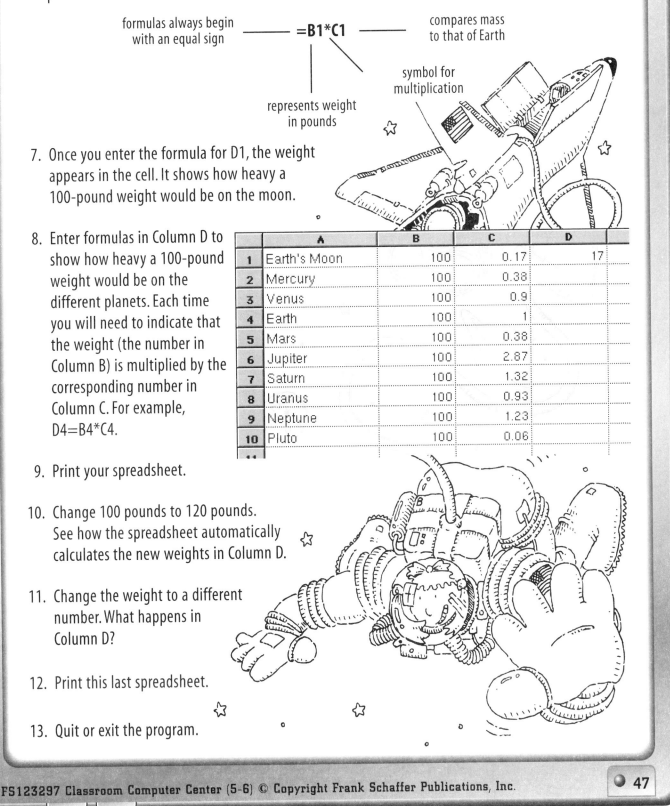

formulas always begin with an equal sign ——— **=B1*C1** ——— compares mass to that of Earth

represents weight in pounds

symbol for multiplication

7. Once you enter the formula for D1, the weight appears in the cell. It shows how heavy a 100-pound weight would be on the moon.

8. Enter formulas in Column D to show how heavy a 100-pound weight would be on the different planets. Each time you will need to indicate that the weight (the number in Column B) is multiplied by the corresponding number in Column C. For example, D4=B4*C4.

	A	B	C	D
1	Earth's Moon	100	0.17	17
2	Mercury	100	0.38	
3	Venus	100	0.9	
4	Earth	100	1	
5	Mars	100	0.38	
6	Jupiter	100	2.87	
7	Saturn	100	1.32	
8	Uranus	100	0.93	
9	Neptune	100	1.23	
10	Pluto	100	0.06	

9. Print your spreadsheet.

10. Change 100 pounds to 120 pounds. See how the spreadsheet automatically calculates the new weights in Column D.

11. Change the weight to a different number. What happens in Column D?

12. Print this last spreadsheet.

13. Quit or exit the program.

Basketball Winnings

Software: *ClarisWorks* Spreadsheet Application (Apple)

Technology Prerequisites: Students must be able to enter formulas and insert headers on spreadsheets.

Content Skills: division, decimals, algebra, sports percentages

Technology Skills: spreadsheet formulas, spreadsheet formats

Lesson Objective

This lesson will give students practice in using spreadsheets to calculate sports percentages. The percentages will reflect the number of games won by basketball teams.

Lesson Plan

1. Ask how many of your students follow sports such as basketball, football, and baseball. Tell the class that although sports differ in many ways, two statistics are part of every team sport—wins and losses. Explain that keeping track of wins and losses helps determine which team has performed the best in a playing season. Then tell students that they will be creating a spreadsheet to see how team standings are calculated in sports.

2. Students begin by selecting the spreadsheet option in *ClarisWorks*. Then have them insert a header by clicking on the *Format* menu and selecting *Insert Header*. Have students title their spreadsheet *Basketball Winnings*. Have them hit the return key and type their name on the second line. Tell students that they will be looking at the statistics of six fictitious basketball teams and comparing them.

3. Explain that in sports, wins and losses are used to calculate a team's winning percentage. Explain that a winning percentage indicates the number of games a team can be expected to win if it played 1,000 games. To determine the winning percentage, the number of wins is divided by the total number of games played (the number of wins and the number of losses). For example, if a team won 9 games and lost 3 games, the winning percentage is calculated by dividing 9 by 12. The winning percentage then would be .750. This means that if the team played 1,000 games, it would be expected to win 750 of them. Point out that the winning percentage is written with three numbers to the right of a decimal.

4. Have students enter these column headings: *Teams* for Column A, *Wins* for Column B, *Losses* for Column C, and *Percentages* for Column D. Next, have them enter the names of the six teams (Dragons, Stars, Titans, Jaguars, Comets, Falcons), beginning with A2 and ending with A7.

	A	B	C	D
1	Teams	Wins	Losses	Percentages
2	Dragons			
3	Stars			
4	Titans			
5	Jaguars			
6	Comets			
7	Falcons			

5. Once students have entered the team names, have them follow the directions on the activity card and input the wins and losses in Columns B and C.

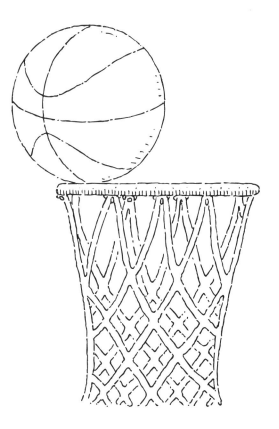

6. Students will need to set up the spreadsheet so that it can calculate the winning percentage. (In *ClarisWorks*, you must indicate how you want the answer to a division problem to be displayed; if you do not do this, the answer may come out with the decimal point in the wrong place.) First, students will highlight the cells in Column D, from D2 to D7. Then they will click on the *Format* menu and select *Number*. A dialog box labeled *Format Number, Date, and Time* will appear. Students will select *Fixed* and click on *3* in the part labeled *Precision*. (This will show the winning percentage as three figures to the right of the decimal point.)

Format Number, Date, and Time	
Number	**Date**
○ General ⌘G	○ 12.23.97 ⌘1
○ Currency ⌘U	○ Dec 23, 1997 ⌘2
○ Percent ⌘P	○ December 23, 1997 ⌘3
○ Scientific ⌘S	○ Tue, Dec 23, 1997 ⌘4
● Fixed ⌘F	○ Tuesday, December 23, 1997 ⌘5
☐ Commas ⌘0	**Time**
☑ Negatives in () ⌘N	○ 01:59 PM ⌘6 ○ 13:59 ⌘7
Precision: 3	○ 01:59:01 PM ⌘8 ○ 13:59:01 ⌘9
?	Apply ⌘Y Cancel ⌘. OK

7. Next, students will enter the formula showing that the number of wins must be divided by the number of games (the number of wins and the number of losses). To do this, they will begin by clicking on D2 and entering **=B2/(B2+C2)**. (Remind the class that formulas begin with an equal sign and that the division sign is indicated by a slash.) The answer that appears in D2 will be the winning percentage for the Dragons (the team listed in A2). Students will continue clicking on each of the remaining cells in Column D and typing the appropriate formula to find the rest of the winning percentages. For example, for D3, they should enter **=B3/(B3+C3)**.

	A	B	C	D
1	Teams	Wins	Losses	Percentages
2	Dragons	35	25	0.583
3	Stars			
4	Titans			
5	Jaguars			
6	Comets			
7	Falcons			

8. Let students add other teams and statistics to the page and calculate winning percentages for them.

9. Tell students to print their spreadsheet.

10. Remind students to quit or exit the program when they are finished so that the computer is ready for the next student.

11. For a follow-up activity, let students look in the newspaper and compare the statistics of their favorite sports teams.

Assessment Criteria

The student set up the spreadsheet correctly.

The student entered data in the appropriate cells.

The student entered the formulas correctly.

	A	B	C	D	
1	Teams	Wins	Losses	Percentages	
2	Dragons	35	25	0.583	
3	Stars	40	28	0.588	
4	Titans	42	23	0.646	
5	Jaguars	48	17	0.738	
6	Comets	28	38	0.424	
7	Falcons	47	19	0.712	

Basketball Winnings

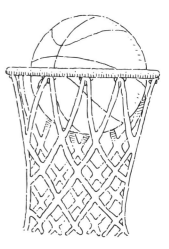

1. Open the *ClarisWorks* program. Select the *Spreadsheet* option.

2. Insert the header. To do this, click on the *Format* menu and select *Insert Header*. Type **Basketball Winnings**. Hit the return key and type your name on the second line.

3. Type the headings for four columns. Type **Teams** in A1, **Wins** in B1, **Losses** C1, and **Percentages** in D1.

4. Enter the team names in Column A. Begin with A2 and end with A7.

Dragons

Stars

Titans

Jaguars

Comets

Falcons

	A	B	C	D	
1	Teams	Wins	Losses	Percentages	
2	Dragons				
3	Stars				
4	Titans				
5	Jaguars				
6	Comets				
7	Falcons				

5. Enter the wins for each team in Column B. Begin with B2 and end with B7. Enter the losses for each team in Column C. Begin with C2 and end with C7.

	Wins	Losses
Dragons	35	25
Stars	40	28
Titans	42	23
Jaguars	48	17
Comets	28	38
Falcons	47	19

	A	B	C	D	
1	Teams	Wins	Losses	Percentages	
2	Dragons	35	25		
3	Stars	40	28		
4	Titans	42	23		
5	Jaguars	48	17		
6	Comets	28	38		
7	Falcons	47	19		

FS123297 Classroom Computer Center (5-6) © Copyright Frank Schaffer Publications, Inc.

reproducible

Basketball Winnings

6. Now you are ready to set up Column D to calculate the teams' winning percentages. First highlight D2 through D8. Click on the *Format* menu and select *Number*. A dialog box will appear. Under the options for *Number*, click on *Fixed*. For *Precision*, click on *3*. Now when you calculate the percentages, you will get three figures to the right of the decimal point (such as 0.583).

Format Number, Date, and Time

Number
- ○ General ⌘G
- ○ Currency ⌘U
- ○ Percent ⌘P
- ○ Scientific ⌘S
- ● Fixed ⌘F
- ☐ Commas ⌘O
- ☑ Negatives in () ⌘N
- Precision: 3

Date
- ○ 12.23.97 ⌘1
- ○ Dec 23, 1997 ⌘2
- ○ December 23, 1997 ⌘3
- ○ Tue, Dec 23, 1997 ⌘4
- ○ Tuesday, December 23, 1997 ⌘5

Time
- ○ 01:59 PM ⌘6   ○ 13:59 ⌘7
- ○ 01:59:01 PM ⌘8   ○ 13:59:01 ⌘9

[?]   [Apply ⌘Y] [Cancel ⌘.] [OK]

7. Click on D2. Enter the formula for calculating the winning percentage for the Dragons:

$$=B2/(B2+C2)$$

The formula shows that the Dragons' number of wins is to be divided by the total number of games played (the number of wins and the number of losses). After you enter the formula, the winning percentage appears in D2.

	A	B	C	D
1	Teams	Wins	Losses	Percentages
2	Dragons	35	25	0.583
3	Stars			
4	Titans			
5	Jaguars			
6	Comets			
7	Falcons			

8. Enter the formulas that will get you the winning percentages for the remaining teams. Remember to begin each formula with an equal sign (=) and to use a slash (/) for division.

9. Add other teams to your spreadsheet. Make up their wins and losses, and calculate their winning percentages.

10. Print your spreadsheet.

11. Quit or exit the program.

reproducible

Software: *ClarisWorks* Painting Application (Apple)

Technology Prerequisites: Students must be able to use the pencil tool and paint tools. They must also be able to change the colors of the paint tools using the color palette.

Content Skills: family crests, self-awareness

Technology Skills: pencil tool, text tool, adding graphics

Lesson Objective

In this lesson, students will design family crests. Each crest will display pictures or symbols that represent a family's background, accomplishments, or interests.

Lesson Plan

1. Tells students that long ago certain families had family crests (a coat of arms). These crests were displayed for identification and for displaying a person's ancestry. Explain that a family crest was shaped like a shield and included colors, patterns, and symbols (such as animals, plants, or objects) that represented the family.

2. Next, have the students share some things about their families' background or interests. For example, they could discuss their countries of origin, special accomplishments, or activities that family members enjoy. Then tell students that they will be using *ClarisWorks* to design a family crest that represents their family's history, values, accomplishments, and/or interests.

3. Students will use the pencil tool and paint tools to make their designs. Remind them that the colors of the tools can be changed by clicking on the color palette.

4. Remind students to type their name at the bottom of the page before printing their work.

5. Remind students to quit or exit the program when they are finished so that the computer is ready for the next student.

Assessment Criteria

The student drew the crest properly.

The student decorated the crest with symbols that represented his or her family.

The student used the pencil tool and paint tools correctly.

A Family Crest

1. Open the *ClarisWorks* program. Select *Painting* option.

2. Select the paintbrush tool. Draw the outline of your crest.

3. Use the paint tools and the pencil tool to decorate your crest. Add pictures that represent your family. For example, you could show symbols that relate to your family's history, values, accomplishments, or interests.

4. Use the color palette to change the colors of the paint tools.

5. Type your name at the bottom of the page.

6. Print.

7. Quit or exit the program.

reproducible

Software: *ClarisWorks* Painting Application (Apple)

Technology Prerequisites: Students must be able to use the text tool, pencil tool, paintbrush, paint can, and spray can. They must also be able to change the colors of the paint tools using the color palette. Students must also be able to use select graphics from the Library and import them into their documents.

Content Skills: westward movement theme, drawing skills

Technology Skills: pencil tool, paint tools (paintbrush, paint can, spray can), color palette, text tool, graphics

Lesson Objective

In this lesson, students will draw a covered wagon. They will also select graphics from the Library and import them into their document.

Lesson Plan

1. Discuss the westward movement with the class, and show pictures of covered wagons from books. Tell students that they will be using *ClarisWorks* to draw a covered wagon for a make-believe journey out west.

2. Instruct the class to use the pencil tool and paint tools to draw a covered wagon at the top-half of the screen.

3. Tell students to add pictures of three items that they would take on their journey. To do this, they will choose graphics from the *Library*. Students will go to the *File* menu and select *Library*. Then they will choose one graphic at a time from the various categories available. When a graphic is selected, they must click on *Use* to place it on their document.

4. Tell students that to move the graphic into place, they must click on it and hold down the mouse while dragging the picture. If they want to change the size of the graphic, they must click on the *Transform* menu while the graphic is still selected (a dashed box appears around the graphic when it is selected) and click on *Resize*. Small boxes will appear at each corner of the

graphic. Students can then click on one of these boxes and drag the mouse until the picture is the desired size. Explain that holding down the shift key while resizing the graphic will keep the picture from becoming distorted.

5. Remind students to type their names at the bottom of the page before printing their work.

6. Remind students to quit or exit the program when they are finished so that the computer is ready for the next student.

Assessment Criteria

The student drew the covered wagon correctly.

The student selected three appropriate graphics.

The student imported, moved, and resized the graphics correctly.

The student used the pencil tool, text tool, and paint tools correctly.

My Covered Wagon

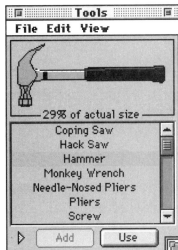

1. Open the *ClarisWorks* program. Select the *Painting* option.

2. Use the paint tools to draw a picture of a covered wagon at the top-half of the screen. Use the color palette to change the tool colors.

3. Insert a graphic of an object you would like to take with you on your wagon. To do this, click on the *File* menu and select *Library*. Click on a category, such as *Food* or *Tools*. Choose the graphic you want and click on *Use*. The graphic will appear on the screen. You will also see a dashed box around the graphic. This box lets you move or change the graphic.

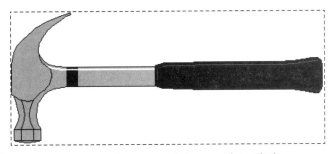

4. Move the graphic where you want it by clicking on it, holding down the mouse, and moving it into place.

5. If you want, resize the graphic at this point. Do this by clicking on the *Transform* menu and selecting *Resize*. You will see four small boxes appear at each corner of the graphic. Click on one of these small boxes, hold down the mouse, and drag the picture to the desired size. To keep the graphic from distorting, hold down the shift key while you resize it.

6. Repeat steps 3–6 and add two more objects you would take on your wagon.

7. Select the text tool. Type your name at the bottom of the page.

8. Print.

9. Quit or exit the program.

reproducible

Software: *ClarisWorks* Painting Application (Apple)

Technology Prerequisites: Students must be able to use the line tool and text tool. They must also be able to import, move, resize, and rotate graphics. They will also need to know how to rotate text.

Content Skills: mapping, community places

Technology Skills: line tool, text tool, graphics

Lesson Objective

Students will draw a community map. They will draw the streets and label them. Students will rotate some of the labels. They will also import graphics from the *Library* and move, resize, and rotate them to fit their maps.

Lesson Plan

1. Discuss with the class the kinds of places that make up a community, such as a bank or a hospital. Tell students that they will be using *ClarisWorks* to make a map.

2. Students will use the line tool to draw the streets. The streets must be at least half an inch wide. They will then use the text tool to label the streets. They will rotate the labels for the vertical streets. To do this, students will select each label with the selection rectangle, click on the *Transform* menu, and select *Rotate*. A dialog box will appear, along with a highlighted box that contains the number 90. Students will click *OK*, and the street name will rotate 90 degrees into vertical position. They will drag the labels into place.

3. Students will use the *Library* to add at least five graphics on their maps. They will click on the *File* menu, select *Library*, and choose pictures from the *Community* category. When students import the graphic onto their document, the picture will appear on the screen with a dashed box around it. This box allows the graphic to be moved or changed.

4. To move the graphic into place, students need to click on the picture and drag it. To resize the graphic, they need to click on the *Transform* menu and select *Resize*. Small boxes will appear on each corner of the graphic. By clicking on a box and dragging the mouse, students can enlarge or reduce the picture. To keep the picture from becoming distorted, they will need to hold down the shift key while resizing.

5. Students can rotate a graphic so that it faces the street properly. To do this, they will need to click on the *Transform* menu and select *Free Rotate*. They can then click on any of the corner boxes to rotate the graphic.

6. Remind students to use the text tool to type their names at the bottom of the page before printing their work. Remind them to quit or exit the program when they are finished.

Assessment Criteria

The student used the line tool and text tool correctly.

The student typed and rotated text appropriately.

The student imported, moved, resized, and rotated the graphics correctly.

A Community Map

1. Open the *ClarisWorks* program. Select the *Painting* option.

2. Use the line tool to draw streets on your map. Make the streets at least half an inch wide. Use the text tool to type the names of the horizontal streets onto your map.

3. Type the names of the vertical streets. To rotate the names, use the selection rectangle (it looks like a dashed box) and select each name one at a time. Click on the *Transform* menu and select *Rotate*. A dialog box will appear and you will see the number 90. Click *OK* and the street name will turn 90 degrees into vertical position. (You will need to repeat this procedure if the street name is not facing the way you want it.)

4. Type your name at the bottom of the page.

5. Insert at least five graphics to represent places on your map. To retrieve a graphic, click on the *File* menu and select *Library*. Then select *Community* to see what graphics are available. Choose one you like and click on *Use*. The graphic will appear on your document with a dashed box around it. This box lets you move or change the graphic.

6. To move a graphic into place, click on it and hold down the mouse as you move the picture. To resize a graphic, click on the *Transform* menu and select *Resize*. Four boxes will appear at each corner of the graphic. Click on one, hold down the mouse, and drag the picture to the desired size. Hold down the shift key while resizing to keep the graphic from becoming distorted.

7. If you like, rotate the graphic so that it faces the street properly. To do this, click on the *Transform* menu and select *Free Rotate*. Click on any one of the four corner boxes that appear around the graphic, and rotate the picture. You may need to move the graphic into place again once it has been rotated.

8. Print.

9. Quit or exit the program.

reproducible

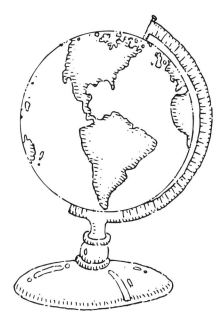

Software: *HyperStudio* (Roger Wagner Publishing)

Technology Prerequisites: Students must be able to use the text tool, pencil tool, paintbrush, and paint can. They need to know how to change the colors of the tools using the color palette. Students must also be able to create new cards and text objects. They must know how to add buttons and transitions.

Content Skills: researching countries, designing brochures

Technology Skills: text tool, pencil tool, paint tools (paintbrush, paint can), color palette, cards, text objects, buttons (including button sounds and text), transitions, special effects

Lesson Objective

In this lesson, students will research a country and create a multimedia travel brochure presenting information about it. This lesson may take several sessions.

Lesson Plan

1. Ask students which countries they would like to visit and why. Then have each student research that country and present the information as a multimedia travel brochure.

2. Tell students that their brochures should contain five cards: a title card, a card displaying a map of the country, a card listing interesting sites, a card discussing culture, and a card presenting travel tips. Encourage the class to use a variety of resources for their research, such as books, CD-ROM programs, and the Internet.

3. Tell students to use the text tool to type the name of the country and their name on the title card. They should also use the paint tools to draw an interesting picture. Remind students that they can change the size and shape of the pencil or paintbrush by clicking on the *Options* menu and selecting *Line Size* or *Brush Shape*.

4. Have students add a button that will let them move from the first card to the second card. To do this, they will need to click on the *Objects* menu and select *Add a Button*. A dialog box will appear. Students will then choose a shape for their button and add a name (the word or phrase that appears on the button). They will also choose the color of the name and the background. When they click *OK*, they will see their button on the card.

5. Once the button appears on their card, students will move it into place by clicking on it and dragging it. Then they will click anywhere on the screen to add actions (sounds and special effects) to the button. A dialog box with two boxes labeled *Places to Go* and *Play a Sound* will appear. In the *Places to Go* box, students will select *Next card*. Another dialog box will appear, and students will choose a transition (a special effect that occurs when moving from one card to the next). When *OK* is clicked, students will return to the previous dialog box.

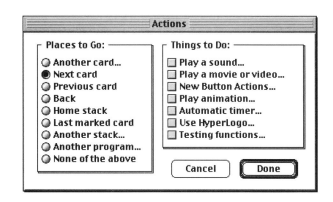

6. Students will click on *Play a Sound* to choose a sound for their button. A dialog box will appear, and students will make their sound selection and click *OK* to return to the previous dialog box. When they click *Done*, they will see their card and the button they created.

7. To add a second card to their stack, students will click on the *Edit* menu and select *New card*. On this card, students will use the paint tools to make a simple map of their country. They will then follow the procedure described in steps 4–6 to add a button to their second card.

8. Students will add a third card that they will use to list interesting sites. To add the card, they will click on the *Edit* menu and select *New card*. They will add a text object (a box or display screen that encloses text) by clicking on the *Objects* menu and selecting *Add a Text Object*. A box (a display screen) will appear on the card. To move it, students will click on it and drag it in place. Then they will click anywhere on the screen to format the text. A dialog box labeled *Text Appearance* will appear, and students will make selections for the color, font, style, size, and alignment of text.

9. Students will need to decide whether to keep the text scrollable. If they are planning to type a lot of text, they should keep the selections *Draw Scroll Bar* and *Scrollable*. (These features are automatically checked off when the *Text Appearance* dialog box appears.) This allows students to type in more text than what appears in their display screen because they are able to scroll through the text. If students are not planning to type much text, they can unselect the scroll features by clicking on the checked boxes.

10. After students type their list of sites, they will use the paint tools to decorate the card.

11. Students will follow the procedure described in the steps above to add the rest of the cards to their stack. The fourth card should present information about the country's culture. The fifth box should give travel tips, such as the kind of weather to expect in that country or the best time to travel there.

12. When adding the button for the fifth card, students will need to indicate that the movement should be from the fifth card to the *first card*, not the next card. To do this, they will need to select *Another card* instead of *Next card* when choosing *Places to Go*. A dialog box with arrows will appear. Students will use the arrows to find the first card in the stack and then click OK. This will "loop" the stack. Have students test their stacks by clicking on *Move* and selecting *First card*. Then they can check their entire presentation by making sure each button works correctly.

13. When students have completed their multimedia brochures, they should save the file as *travel.their initials*.

14. Remind students to quit or exit the program when they are finished. If you have a large screen projection device (see page 2), allow students to share their multimedia presentations to the class.

Assessment Criteria

The student presented accurate information about a country.

The student correctly created the cards, added buttons and text and looped the cards.

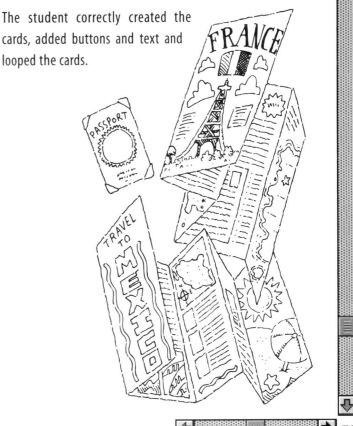

Multimedia Travel Brochure

1. Open the *HyperStudio* program. Select *New Stack*.

2. The first card will be your title card. Use the text tool to type the name of the country and your name on the card. Use the paint tools to draw a picture representing the country.

3. Add a button to the card. To do this, click on the *Objects* menu and select *Add a Button*. A dialog box will appear. Choose a shape for the button. Then type a name for the button in the *Name* box. (The name is the word or phrase that you want to see on the button.)

4. Click on the color boxes and choose a color for the name and for the background. Click *OK*.

5. The button will appear on the first card. Move it by clicking on it and dragging it into place. Then click anywhere on the screen. A dialog box labeled *Actions* will appear. It lets you choose actions for your button.

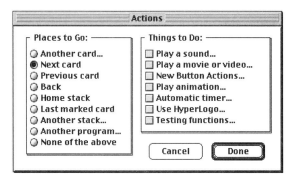

6. In the *Places to Go* box, select *Next card*. A dialog box labeled *Transitions* will appear. Choose a transition and then click *OK*. You will get back to the dialog box labeled *Actions*.

7. Click on *Play a Sound* in the *Things to Do* box. Then choose a sound for your button. If you want to hear the sound, click on *Play*. When you are finished, click *OK* to get back to the *Actions* dialog box. Then click *Done* to get back to the first card.

8. Add your second card by clicking on the *Edit* menu and selecting *New card*. Use the paint tools to draw a simple map of the country. Then follow steps 3–8 to add a button that lets you move to your third card.

9. Add the third card by clicking on the *Edit* menu and selecting *New card*. You will be typing a list of interesting sites on this card. First, you will need to add a text object. To do this, click on the *Objects* menu and selecting *Add a Text Object*. A box will appear. You will use this box (a display screen) to hold your text. To move the box, click on it and drag it into place. Click anywhere on the screen. You will see a dialog box labeled *Text Appearance*.

Multimedia Travel Brochure

10. Do not type anything in the Name box, but pick a color for the text and the background.

11. If you see the options *Draw Scroll Bar* and *Scrollable* checked off, it means you will be able to keep on typing even after the box holding your text looks "filled." That is because as you enter more text, you can scroll (move) down to see more of it. If you think you will not be typing a lot of text, unselect the scroll feature by clicking on the checked boxes beside *Draw Scroll Bar* and *Scrollable*. The text will then be unscrollable—that means you can only type what will fit in the box.

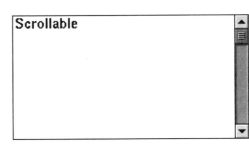

12. To format the text, click on *Style*. You will see a dialog box with options for font, style, size, and alignment of text. Make your selections and then click *OK*. You will get back to the previous dialog box. Click *OK* to return to your card. Then type a list of interesting sites. When you are finished, use the paint tools to decorate the card.

13. Follow steps 3–8 to add a button that lets you move to the fourth card.

14. Add your fourth card by clicking on the *Edit* menu and selecting *New card*. This card should present information about the country's culture. Follow steps 9–12 to type the text. Then follow steps 3–8 to add a button that lets you move to the fifth card.

15. Add the fifth card. This card should present travel tips such as the kind of weather to expect or the kind of currency used. Follow steps 9–12 to add the text and pictures.

16. Add a button to your fifth card by following steps 3–8, but choose the sound before the transition. Then select *Another card* instead of *Next card* for *Places to Go*. A dialog box with arrows will appear. Click on the arrows until you get to the first card in your stack. Then click *OK*. This will "loop" the cards in the stack.

17. Test your stack by clicking on *Move* and selecting *First card*. Go through your stack and check each button.

18. Save the file as **travel.your initials**.

19. Quit or exit the program.

reproducible

Software: *HyperStudio* (Roger Wagner Publishing)

Technology Prerequisites: Students must be able to use the text tool, pencil tool, paintbrush, and paint can. They need to know how to change colors of the tools using the color palette. Students must also be able to create new cards and text objects. They must know how to add buttons and transitions.

Content Skills: inventions, science history, technological advances

Technology Skills: text tool, pencil tool, paint tools (paintbrush, paint can), color palette, cards, text objects, buttons (including button sounds and text), transitions, special effects

Lesson Objective

In this lesson, students will present information about an invention and discuss how it has influenced people's lives.

Lesson Plan

1. Ask students to name important inventions. List their ideas on the chalkboard. Then tell them that they will be researching an invention of their choice and creating a multimedia report about it.

2. Tell students that they will be using *HyperStudio* to create three cards: the first card will include a picture and a description of the invention; the second card will display a sketch of the inventor and a sentence telling when the invention was made; the third card will describe how the invention affected people's lives.

3. For the first card, students will use the pencil tool and paint tools to draw the invention. Remind students that they can change the size and shape of the pencil or paintbrush by clicking on the *Options* menu and selecting *Line Size* or *Brush Shape*.

4. Students will add a text object (a box or display screen that encloses text) by clicking on the *Objects* menu and selecting *Add a Text Object*. A box, or display screen, will appear on the card. To move it, students will click on it and drag it in place. Then they will click anywhere on the screen to format the text. A dialog box labeled *Text*

Appearance will appear, and students will make selections for the color, font, style, size, and alignment of text. Afterwards, students can type a description of the invention on the card.

5. Next, students will add a button to move to the second card. To do this, they will click on the *Objects* menu and select *Add a Button*. A dialog box labeled *Button Appearance* will appear. Students will choose a shape for their button.

6. Students will add a graphic, rather than a name, to their button. On the *Button Appearance* dialog box, they will see a box checked off beside the label *Show Name*. They need to click on this box to deselect it; then they will click on the *Show Icon* box to access the graphics. Students will select the picture they want and click *OK*. The graphic will appear on the button.

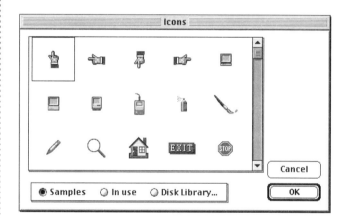

7. Students will then choose the background color of the button. When students click *OK*, the button will appear on the card. To move it, they must click on it and drag it. Then they will click anywhere on the screen to add actions (sounds and special effects) to the button.

8. An *Actions* dialog box will appear, with selections for *Places to Go* and *Play a Sound*. For *Places to Go*, students will select *Next card*. A *Transitions* dialog box will appear, and students will choose a transition (a special effect that occurs when moving from one card to the next).

9. Students will click on *Play a Sound* to choose a sound for their button. A dialog box will appear, and students will make their sound selection and click *OK* to return to the previous dialog box. When they click *Done*, they will see their card and the button they created.

10. To add a second card, students will click on the *Edit* menu and select *New card*. They will use the pencil tool and paint tools to draw a picture of the inventor; they will use the text tool to type the inventor's name and add a sentence about when the invention was made. Students will then follow the procedure described in the steps above to add a button to move to the third card.

11. Students will add a third card by clicking on the *Edit* menu and selecting *New card*. They will also add a text object as described above. On this card, students will type a paragraph discussing how the invention influenced people's lives.

12. When adding the button for the third card, students will need to indicate that the movement should be from the third card to the first card, not the next card. To do this, they will need to select *Another card* instead of *Next card* when choosing *Places to Go*. A dialog box with arrows will appear. Students will use the arrows to find the first card in the stack and then click *OK*. This will "loop" the stack. Have students test their stacks by clicking on *Move* and selecting *First card*. Then they can check their presentation by making sure each button works correctly.

13. When students have completed their reports, they should save the file as *invent.their initials*.

14. Remind students to quit or exit the program when they are finished. If you have a large screen projection device (see page 2), let students show their multimedia presentations to the class.

Assessment Criteria

The student presented accurate information about the invention.

The student created the cards correctly.

The student added buttons correctly.

The student added text correctly.

The student looped the cards correctly.

Fabulous Inventions

1. Open the *HyperStudio* program. Select *New Stack*.

2. You will see your first card. Use the paint tools to draw a picture of the invention you chose.

3. Add a text object by clicking on the *Objects* menu and selecting *Add a Text Object*. A box will appear. This box will hold your text. To move it, click on it and drag it into place. Click anywhere on the screen. You will see a dialog box labeled *Text Appearance*.

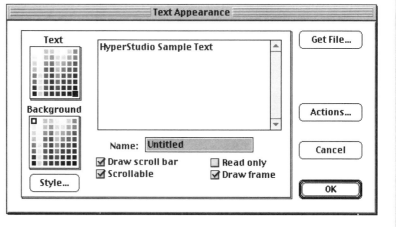

4. Do not type anything in the *Name* box, but pick a color for the text and the background.

5. To format the text, click on *Style*. You will see a dialog box with options for font, style, size, and alignment of text. Make your selections and then click *OK*. You will get back to the previous dialog box. Click *OK* to return to your card. Then type a description of the invention.

6. Add a button by clicking on the *Objects* menu and selecting *Add a Button*. A dialog box labeled *Button Appearance* will appear. Choose a shape for the button.

7. You will be adding a graphic instead of a name to the button. You will see a checked box labeled *Show Name*. Click on this box to deselect it. Then add a graphic by clicking on the *Show Icon* box. Graphics will appear. Click on the picture you want and click *OK*. The picture will appear on the button.

Fabulous Inventions

8. Choose a color for the background of the button by clicking on the color box. Click *OK*. Your button will appear on the first card.

9. Move the button by clicking on it and dragging it into place. Then click anywhere on the screen. A dialog box labeled *Actions* will appear. It lets you choose actions for your button.

10. In the *Places to Go* box, select *Next card* to get the *Transitions* dialog box. Choose a transition and then click *OK*. You will get back to the *Actions* dialog box.

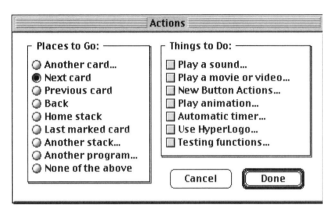

11. Click on *Play a Sound* in the *Things to Do* box. Then choose a sound for your button. If you want to hear the sound, click on *Play*. When you are finished, click *OK* to get back to the *Actions* dialog box. Then click *Done* to get back to the first card.

12. Add your second card by clicking on the *Edit* menu and selecting *New card*. Use the paint tools to draw the inventor. Use the text tool to type the inventor's name. Add a sentence about when he or she made the invention. Follow steps 6–11 to add a button that lets you move to your third card.

13. On the third card, you will type a paragraph describing how the invention influenced people's lives. Follow steps 3–5 to add your text.

14. Add a button to your third card by following steps 6–11, but choose the sound before the transition. Then select *Another card* instead of *Next card* for *Places to Go*. A dialog box with arrows will appear. Click on the arrows until you get to the first card in your stack. Then click *OK*. This will "loop" the cards in the stack.

15. Test your stack by clicking on *Move* and selecting *First card*. Go through your stack and check each button.

16. Save the file as **invent.your initials**.

17. Quit or exit the program.

A Look at Molecules

Software: *ClarisWorks* Painting Application (Apple)

Technology Prerequisites: Students must be able to use the oval tool, paint can, and text tool. They also must know how to change the colors of the tools using the color palette.

Content Skills: matter, molecules

Technology Skills: oval tool, paint can, color palette, text tool, formatting text

Lesson Objective

In this lesson, students will learn that molecules are the basic units of matter. They will use *ClarisWorks* to draw simple molecular structures.

Lesson Plan

1. Pour some water from a glass into a small cup. Next, use an eyedropper to draw some of the water from the cup. Place a drop on a piece of wax paper. Ask the students what they think is the smallest amount of water they could get. Then tell them that the smallest particle into which water can be divided into (and still be considered water) is called a molecule. Point out that a drop of water contains billions of water molecules.

2. Tell the class that molecules are made up of smaller units called atoms. Explain that atoms form substances called chemical elements. These elements include oxygen, hydrogen, and iron. Each of these elements is made up of one kind of atom. Tell the class that different kinds of

atoms link together to form molecules; for example, two hydrogen atoms link up with one oxygen atom to form a water molecule.

3. Tell students that they will be drawing one or more simple molecules. Explain that atoms join to one another in different ways; some form straight lines, others make zigzag patterns, and some form bulbous structures. Have students look at some models you've prepared ahead of time to make their drawings. (See the drawings on this page.)

4. Students will use the shape tools to draw the atoms. They will use the paint can to color each kind of atom a different color. They will label the atoms and the molecules using the text tool. To boldface a word, students will need to select it, click on *Style*, and select *Bold*.

5. Remind students to use the text tool to type their names at the bottom of the page before printing their work.

6. Remind students to quit or exit the program when they are finished.

Assessment Criteria

The student used the oval tool and paint can correctly.

The student used the text tool correctly.

The student labeled the picture correctly.

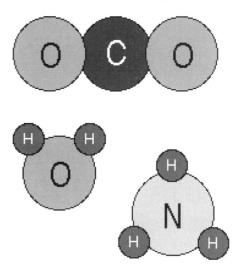

A Look at Molecules

1. Open the *ClarisWorks* program. Select the *Painting* option.

2. Select the oval tool. Draw the different atoms to make the molecule.

3. Use the paint can to color the atoms. Make each kind of atom a different color.

4. Use the text tool to label each atom.

5. Type the name of the molecule below its picture. Then **boldface** the name. To do this, click on the *Style* menu and select *Bold*.

6. Make another molecule if you like.

7. Use the text tool to type your name at the bottom of the page.

8. Print.

9. Quit or exit the program.

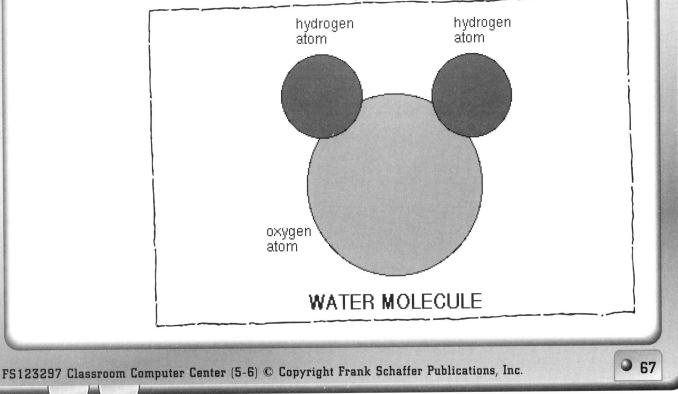

hydrogen atom

hydrogen atom

oxygen atom

WATER MOLECULE

Software: *ClarisWorks* Painting Application (Apple)

Technology Prerequisites: Students must be able to use the text tool, paintbrush, paint can, and color palette. They also need to know how to change the size and style of text.

Content Skills: simple machines, observation

Technology Skills: text tool, paint can, color palette, formatting text

Lesson Objective

Students will review simple machines and look for examples of them in their home. Then they will use ClarisWorks to present what they found.

Lesson Plan

1. Discuss simple machines and how they work:

   Lever—is a bar that rests on a support; when force is applied to one end, a load is lifted at the other end

   Wheel and axle—transports loads by rolling rather than sliding

   Pulley—consists of a wheel with a grooved rim over which a rope passes

   Ramp—is an inclined plane that makes it easier to slide a load upward

   Screw—is a spiraled inclined plane that lets you move a load

   Wedge—is an inclined plane that is driven into another object

   Afterwards, have the class look around the school for examples of these simple machines. (Examples: lever—scissors, wheel and axle—car; pulley—flagpole; ramp—dustpan; screw—screw on switchplate; wedge—knife)

2. For a homework assignment, have students look in their homes for examples of simple machines. Tell them to make a list of the items they find and to return the list to school.

3. Have students use the painting feature in *ClarisWorks* to display their findings. Tell students to use the text tool to type the name of each simple machine and the various examples. Have students use the *Style* menu to boldface the name of each simple machine.

4. After students have finished their list, have them use the paint tools to draw some of the items on the page.

5. Remind students to type their names at the bottom of the page before printing their work.

6. Remind students to quit or exit the program when they are finished.

Assessment Criteria

The student listed appropriate examples of simple machines.

The student used the text tool correctly.

The students used the paint tools correctly.

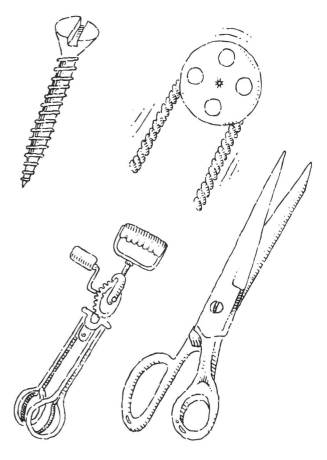

Simple Machines

1. Open the *ClarisWorks* program. Select the *Painting* option.

2. Select the text tool. Type the name of each simple machine. Below each name, type some examples.

3. Make the name of each simple machine bold. To do this, use the selection rectangle (it looks like a dashed box) and select the name you want. Then click on the *Style* menu and select *Bold*. Repeat this activity for each of the other names.

4. Use the paintbrush to draw at least one example of each simple machine. Color the objects by using the paint can and color palette.

5. Type your name at the bottom of the page.

6. Print.

7. Quit or exit the program.

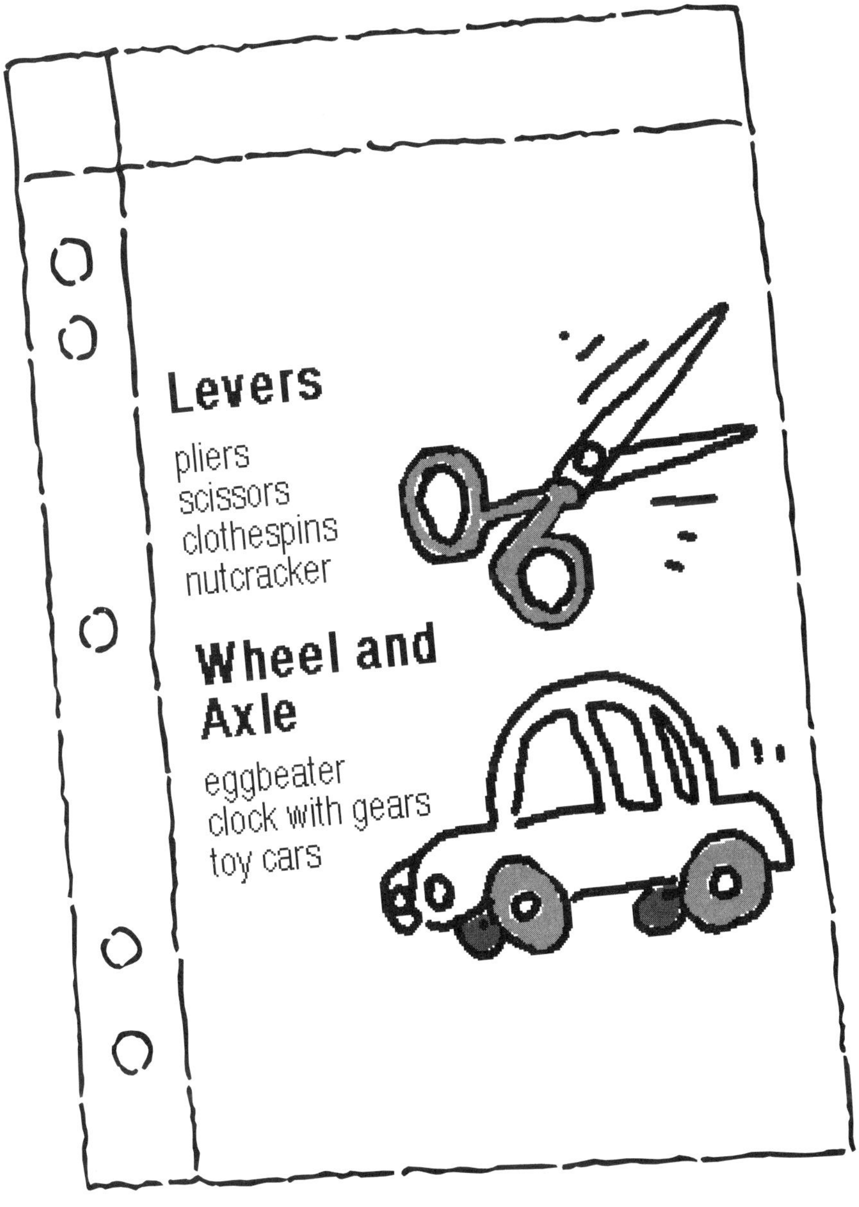

Levers

pliers
scissors
clothespins
nutcracker

Wheel and Axle

eggbeater
clock with gears
toy cars

reproducible

Software: *ClarisWorks* Painting Application (Apple)

Technology Prerequisites: Students must be able to use the rectangle tool, line tool, and text tool.

Content Skills: breathing rates, respiration, making a chart

Technology Skills: rectangle tool, line tool, text tool

Lesson Objective

Students will learn that people have different breathing rates. They will also see that vigorous activity influences the rate at which we breathe. Students will make a chart in *ClarisWorks* to present their findings.

Lesson Plan

1. Ask your students if they think everyone breathes at the same rate. To check their ideas, time the students for 15 seconds while they breathe normally and count their breaths. (One inhale and exhale count as one breath.) Then have them multiply their results by 4 to get breaths per minute. Record the numbers on the chalkboard, and have the class compare the results. (The numbers will vary.)

2. Tell each student to record his or her breathing rate (breaths per minute) on a sheet of paper. Next, ask the students what they think happens to the breathing rates when they exercise. Then time them for one minute as they run in place. Immediately after, have each student count his or her breaths for 15 seconds and calculate the breathing rate. Tell the students to record their rates on their papers.

3. Have students rest for 15 minutes, and then let them calculate their breathing rates again. They will discover that breathing rates increased when they ran and decreased when they rested. Explain that this happened because their body needed to take in more fuel (oxygen) when they were running. When their body no longer needed the extra fuel, their breathing rate slowed down.

4. Have students record their findings by making a chart in *ClarisWorks*. Have the students use the rectangle tool to make a white box. (The box will need to be white.) Have the class use the line tool to divide the box into columns and rows. Then students will use the text tool to type the headings and record their breathing rates.

5. Remind students to type their names at the bottom of the page before printing their work.

6. Remind students to quit or exit the program when they are finished. Later, let the class compare the charts to see how much the breathing rates varied.

Assessment Criteria

The student drew the chart properly.

The student used the rectangle tool and line tool correctly.

The student added text onto the chart correctly.

Breathing Rates

1. Open the *ClarisWorks* program. Select the *Painting* option.

2. You will be making a chart to show what your breathing rate is in different situations. To begin, select the rectangle tool. Make sure the color palette shows white. Then draw a large rectangle that fills a little more than half the screen.

3. Select the line tool. Divide the rectangle into three columns. Your first column (on the left) will be a little narrower than the other two columns. Then use the line tool to divide the chart into four rows. The top row will be about half the width of the other columns.

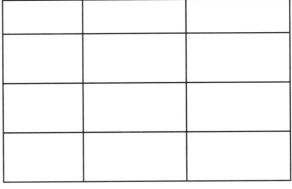

4. Select the text tool. Label the top of the middle column **Breaths in 15 Seconds**. Label the column at the right **Breaths in 1 Minute**.

5. Label the rows. You will skip the first row. Label the second row **At rest**. Label the third row **After running in place for 1 minute**. Label the third row **After resting again for 15 minutes**.

6. Use the text tool to fill in the chart.

7. Type your name at the bottom of the page.

8. Print.

9. Quit or exit the program.

	Breaths in 15 Seconds	Breaths in 1 Minute
At rest		
After running in place for 1 minute		
After resting again for 15 minutes		

reproducible

Software: *ClarisWorks* Painting Application (Apple)

Technology Prerequisites: Students must be able to use the oval tool, line tool, and text tool. They also need to know how to format text (change size and style). They will need to use the selection rectangle to center text.

Content Skills: ocean, Earth's resources, making a web

Technology Skills: oval tool, line tool, text tool, selection rectangle, formatting text

Lesson Objective
In this lesson, students will create a web to illustrate the various kinds of resources we get from the ocean.

Lesson Plan
1. Discuss with the class that the ocean is an important source of food, minerals, and other resources. Then have the students research three kinds of products that we get from the sea. (Examples: food—fish, shellfish; minerals—salt, sand; energy—petroleum, natural gas; medicines—anticoagulants; jewelry—pearls, shells)

   Tell students that they will use *ClarisWorks* to create a web showing three kinds of products that come from the sea.

2. Tell students to use the oval tool to make an oval at the top of the screen, in the center of the page. Students will then use the text tool to type *Ocean* inside the oval. They will use the *Size* menu to change the type to 18-point and the *Style* menu to boldface the word. They will use the selection rectangle to center the word.

3. Have students draw three more ovals across the screen, below the first oval. They should use the text tool to label these ovals with the kinds of products they will display on the web, such as *Food*, *Minerals*, and *Energy*. Students will change the size of the type to 18-point, but they will not need to boldface these headings.

4. Tell students to add more ovals below each heading, and on each one type specific examples of the products, such as shellfish for the food category.

5. Have students use the line tool to connect the ovals to complete their webs.

6. Remind students to quit or exit the program when they are finished so that the computer is ready for the next student.

Assessment Criteria
The student drew the web properly.

The student chose appropriate products.

The student used the oval tool, line tool, and text tool correctly.

The student formatted the text correctly.

Resources from the Sea

1. Open the *ClarisWorks* program. Select the *Painting* option.

2. Select the oval tool and draw an oval in the middle of the page, at the top of the screen. Use the text tool to type **Ocean** inside the oval. Then highlight the word. Click on the *Size* menu and select *18 point* for the type. Click on the *Style* menu and select *Bold*.

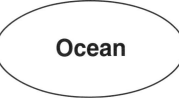

3. You may need to center *Ocean* inside the oval. To do this, click on the selection rectangle. (It looks like a dashed box.) Select *Ocean* and move the word until it is centered.

4. Use the oval tool to draw three more ovals across the page, just below the first one you made. Use the text tool to type the names of three kinds of products that come from the ocean. Each time, highlight the word, click on the *Size* menu and select *18 point*. You do not need to make these labels bold.

5. Follow the procedure described in step 3 to center the words if necessary.

6. Use the oval tool to draw more ovals below each category. Then use the text tool to type specific examples of the products.

7. Use the line tool to connect the ovals.

8. Type your name at the bottom of the page.

9. Print.

10. Quit or exit the program.

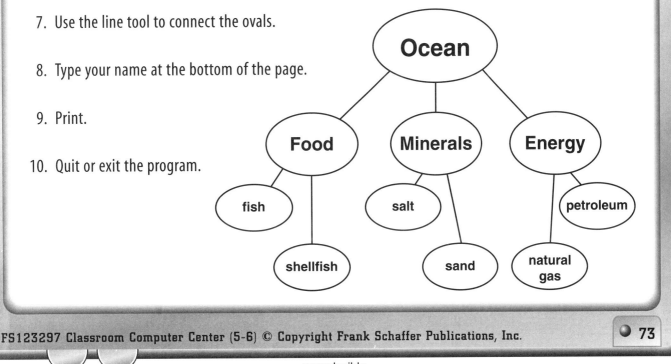

reproducible

Software: *HyperStudio* (Roger Wagner Publishing)

Technology Prerequisites: Students must be able to use the paint tools and change the tool colors using the color palette. They must also be able to create cards, copy cards, add buttons, and add transitions.

Content Skills: ocean life, art

Technology Skills: paint tools (paintbrush, paint can), color palette, cards, buttons, transitions, copying cards

Lesson Objective

Students will create four scenes by adding layers of pictures to one basic scene. They will add buttons to each card so that when they are pressed, the scenes move from one to another to create a "movie."

Lesson Plan

1. Tell students that they will be creating a multimedia presentation of underwater scenes. Explain that each scene will be built upon the previous one so that the sequence of pictures form a "movie."

2. Tell students that their presentations will consist of four cards. The first card will show an underwater scene with no animals. The second card will show one or two sea creatures added to the scene. The third card will show more animals. The fourth card will show even more creatures and perhaps a submarine. When the sequence of cards is played, the effect will be that of creatures moving towards one spot in the ocean.

3. Have students begin by creating the first card and using the paint tools to make a scene. They will also add a button to the card. The button will be labeled **1** and placed at one of the top corners of the picture.

4. Students will follow the procedures outlined on their activity card to add sounds and special effects to their button. To do this, they will access the *Actions* dialog box. They will need to make selections for *Places to Go* and *Play a Sound*. For *Places to Go*, they will select *Next card*.

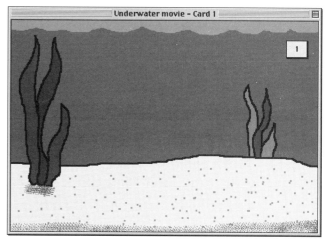

A *Transitions* dialog box will appear, and they will choose a transition (a special effect that occurs when they press the button and move from one card to the next). Students will click *OK* to get back to the *Actions* dialog box. Then they will choose a sound. When students click *Done*, their first card will reappear on the screen.

5. Next, students will copy the first card by clicking on the *Edit* menu and selecting *Copy card*. They will then click on the *Edit* menu again and select *Paste card*. The second card automatically appears on the screen.

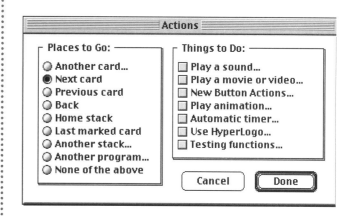

6. The second card will look just like the first card. Students will use the paint tools to add one or two sea creatures to the scene. Then they will add a button and label it **2**. The button should be placed below the first button. After students add a sound and a special effect to their button, they will copy the second card by clicking on the *Edit* menu and selecting *Copy card*. They will then click on the *Edit* menu again and select *Paste card*. The third card automatically appears on the screen.

7. Students will continue following the previous procedure to add two more cards to their stack. The button for the third card should be labeled **3**. The button for the fourth card should be labeled **4**.

8. When students are ready to add a sound effect to their fourth button, the procedure changes slightly. Unlike the other cards, students will need to choose the sound before the transition. After they choose a sound, they will go to the box labeled *Places to Go*. Instead of *Next card*, students will select *Another card*. A dialog box with arrows will appear. Students will use the arrows to find the first card in the stack and then click *OK*. This will "loop" the stack.

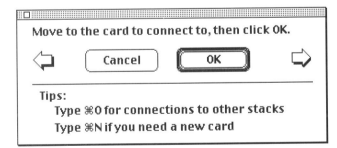

9. Have students test their stacks by clicking on *Move* and selecting *First card*. Then they can check their presentation by making sure each button works correctly.

10. When students have completed their work, they should save the file as *sea.their initials*.

11. Remind students to quit or exit the program when they are finished. If you have a large screen projection device (see page 2), let students show their multimedia presentations to the class.

Assessment Criteria

The student created the cards correctly.

The student added buttons and button features correctly.

The student copied the cards correctly.

The student looped the cards correctly.

Underwater Scenes

1. Open the *HyperStudio* program. Select *New Stack*.

2. You will see your first card. Use the paint tools to draw an undersea picture. Do not draw any sea creatures on this card.

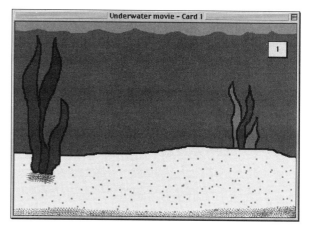

3. Add a button to the card by clicking on the *Objects* menu and selecting *Add a Button*. A dialog box labeled *Button Appearance* will appear. Choose a shape for the button.

4. Type **1** in the *Name* box. Choose a color for the text and background of the button. Click *OK*. Your button will appear on the first card.

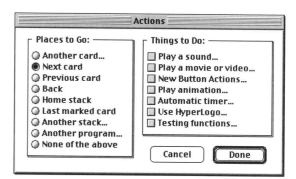

5. Move the button by clicking on it and dragging it into place. For this project, it's best to place the button at one of the top corners of the page. Then click anywhere on the screen. A dialog box labeled *Actions* will appear. It lets you choose actions for the button.

6. In the *Places to Go* box, select *Next card*. You will see a *Transitions* dialog box. Choose a transition and then click *OK*. You will get back to the *Actions* dialog box.

7. Click on *Play a Sound* in the *Things to Do* box. Then choose a sound for your button. If you want to hear the sound, click on *Play*. When you are finished, click *OK* to get back to the *Actions* dialog box. Then click *Done* to get back to the first card.

8. To create your second card, you will need to copy the first card. To do this, click on the *Edit* menu and select *Copy card*. Then click on the *Edit* menu again and select *Paste card*.

9. Your second card automatically appears on the screen. It will look just like the first card. Use the paint tools to add one or two fish to the picture.

FS123297 Classroom Computer Center (5-6) © Copyright Frank Schaffer Publications, Inc.

reproducible

Underwater Scenes

10. Follow steps 3–7 to add the button to your second card. Name the button **2**, and place it below the first button.

11. To create your third card, you will need to copy the second card. To do this, click on the *Edit* menu and select *Copy card*. (Since your second card is still on the screen, that is the card that will be copied.) Then click on the *Edit* menu again and select *Paste card*.

12. Your third card automatically appears. It will look just like the second card. Use the paint tools to add other animals to the picture.

13. Follow steps 3–7 to add the button to your third card. Name the button **3**, and place it below the second button.

14. To create your fourth card, you will need to copy the third card. To do this, click on the *Edit* menu and select *Copy card*. Then click on the *Edit* menu again and select *Paste card*.

15. Your fourth card automatically appears. It will look just like the third card. Use the paint tools to add a submarine or other interesting item to the picture.

16. Add a button to your fourth card by following step 3 and naming the button **4**. Place the button below the third button. Follow steps 4–7, but choose the sound before the transition. Then select *Another card* instead of *Next card* for *Places to Go*. A dialog box with arrows will appear. Click on the arrows until you get to the first card in your stack. Then click *OK*. This will "loop" the cards in the stack.

17. Test your stack by clicking on *Move* and selecting *First card*. Go through your stack and check each button.

18. Save the file as **sea.yourinitials**.

19. Quit or exit the program.

reproducible

Congratulations!

_____

is a
Computer Whiz

FS123297 Classroom Computer Center (5-6) © Copyright Frank Schaffer Publications, Inc.